# Beyond the Scar

## Healing the Wounds of Trauma

**Dr. Steve West**

# PRAISE FOR BEYOND THE SCAR

Beyond the Scar is a courageous and deeply personal offering from a veteran, chaplain, and faithful follower of Christ. With pastoral tenderness and lived vulnerability, Steve shares his journey through PTSD not as a story of easy resolution, but as a testament to God's patient, redemptive work. He invites us to name our wounds and to pursue healing without shame. Through powerful storytelling and spiritual insight, he reminds us that we are not alone. In a world full of darkness, Steve's book is a sacred companion for the road toward the Light.

—Rev. Dr. Nicole Massie Martin, Author of *Nailing It: Why Successful Leadership Demands Suffering and Surrender*

*Beyond the Scar* is a powerful, grace-filled journey into the heart of trauma and the hope of healing. With unflinching honesty and sacred compassion, this book names the wounds we carry, the questions we fear, and the God who meets us there. Every chapter is a lifeline for the hurting—and a gentle guide for those walking beside them. West threads the needle by tackling a subject we too often ignore.

— Philip E. Dearborn, Ed.D., President, Association of Biblical Higher Education

*Beyond the Scar* echoes the inspiring words of an athletics coach that dominate my thoughts every time I lace up my running shoes: 'You haven't come this far to only get this far.' In trauma, as in athletics, you decide if the agonizing pain you experience along the way is an excuse to quit or a catalyst to keep going. Whether the scar is on your body or on your soul, you can move past the events that caused your pain to a victory you could never have imagined. Having gone beyond his own scars while still acknowledging their lingering presence, Steve West shows you how to do the same.

—Dondi E. Costin, PhD, President, Liberty University, Major General, U.S. Air Force (Retired)

In this compassionate and deeply redemptive book, Chaplain Steve West holds out the hope of healing to those who suffer trauma's many harms. Written by a man who has experienced the healing of his own hurts, *Beyond the Scar* will help both survivors and their caregivers understand the pains of trauma more comprehensively and receive the loving mercy of Jesus.

—Dr. Philip Graham Ryken, President, Wheaton College

*Beyond the Scar* is a powerful reminder that God can bring purpose from our pain. Dr. Steve West shares his journey through trauma with honesty and hope, showing how our scars can become tools to help others heal. This book is an encouragement to anyone facing hardship, offering faith, strength, and a renewed sense of direction.

—Valerie Dowling, Director, Women's Democracy Network, International Republican Institute

In our fast-paced, quick-fix, 'pull yourself up by your bootstraps' culture, *Beyond the Scar* offers a much-needed invitation to slow down and truly heal. As a therapist who specializes in trauma for both civilian and responder communities—and as someone who has personally experienced its impact—I can say without hesitation that this book is a must-read. Dr. Steve West gives trauma a voice and offers a clear, compassionate path forward. His honest reflections, combined with an accessible explanation of how trauma affects the brain and body, create space for readers to feel, process, and ultimately heal. Through God, supportive relationships, and personal surrender, healing becomes not only possible, but within reach.

— Kelli Mosley, Licensed Marriage and Family Therapist

Few books have the power to walk tenderly into the sacred space of trauma and meet people with both truth and grace. *Beyond the Scar* by Dr. Steve West does just that. With pastoral compassion and clinical wisdom, Dr. West invites readers on a journey of healing—one marked not by quick fixes or religious clichés, but by presence, process, and the power of God's nearness.

—Brandon Doss, M.Div, Lead Team Pastor, Cultivate Church

Steve West pulls back the curtain on the sometimes emotionally crippling effect of unresolved trauma returning under the surface for believers who are often conditioned to think it should be suppressed. As Steve reveals, there are different levels of mental/emotional trauma, but thank goodness he lays out the Scripturally-based blueprint to help us navigate it for our growth.

—Mike Dubberly, Co-anchor of Good Day Alabama on WBRC TV 6 News

The value and impact of hope is one that cannot possibly be measured. Steve's life of service, intention, and faith on display is a beacon of hope for those of us lucky enough to know him. Now, through *Beyond the Scar*, readers are invited into that same gift. This book is the very fruit of scars, not erased, but transformed; failures, not shamed, but commissioned; pain, not in vain, but purposed. This book is a beautiful resource that marries experience, Bliblical insight and a deep understanding of the psychology of PTSD. A must read for anyone searching for hope.

—Becca Poe, MA, LPC, Licensed Professional Counselor, Owner, Confident Hope LLC

# Beyond The Scar

Healing The Wounds of Trauma

Published by C&S Publishing, Pelham, Alabama

ISBN    (Paperback): 979-8-9891246-3-3

ISBN    (Hardback): 979-8-9891246-4-0

ISBN    (EPub): 979-8-9891246-5-7

Printed in the United States of America

# Disclaimer

The information provided in this book is designed to provide helpful information on the subjects discussed. This book is not meant to be used, nor should it be used, to diagnose or treat any medical condition. For diagnosis or treatment of any medical problem, consult your own physician.

*All scriptures used in this book are from the English Standard Version (ESV) unless otherwise stated.

TO CONTACT THE AUTHOR: www.steve@drstevewest.com

# Dedication

To the wounded who keep walking,

the silent sufferers, the ones who smile while breaking inside, this book is for you.

To every trauma survivor who has felt unseen, unheard, and alone:

you are not beyond healing. Your scars do not disqualify you. They testify to your strength.

And to the caregivers, chaplains, pastors, and friends who walk with the hurting,

your presence is sacred. Thank you for standing in the gap.

# TABLE OF CONTENTS

 ACKNOWLEDGMENTS

This book was born out of both deep pain and deeper grace.

To the many individuals who trusted me with your stories, thank you. You are the heartbeat of these pages. Your honesty, courage, and resilience are sacred. I've carried your voices with me in every chapter.

To Cherri, my wife and constant companion, you are my long time sojourner. Thank you for your patience, your prayers, and your belief in this message and in me.

To Adam and Jennifer, my children. You inspire me more than you know. Your love, strength, and laughter remind me daily that healing is not only possible; it is beautiful.

To Meredith Dunn and Wendy Walters. Thank you for your skillful assistance in the technical and editorial work of preparing this manuscript for publication. Your professionalism, insight, and steady presence helped bring clarity and structure to what God had placed on my heart.

To the friends who encouraged me along the way; even when you didn't realize you were doing it—thank you. Your kindness, prayers, and simple presence often arrived at just the right time.

And above all, to Jesus; my Redeemer, my Shepherd, my Healer. You walked with me through the fire. You carried me when I could not walk. This book is my offering of gratitude to the One who makes all things new.

 FOREWORD

For many years on my office desk has been a piece of art given to me by some colleagues. The small, delicate bowl is made in the *Kintsugi* style, which means "gold mending" in Japanese. It is the craft of mending broken pottery by rejoining the various shards with lacquer and powdered gold or silver. The artist doesn't hide the imperfections but rather embraces the fractures and illuminates them with golden or silvery seams. Brokenness is not rejected but remade.

Sometimes during the day, I will pause from the work of ministry to look at this bowl and remember that Jesus himself became a wounded healer and that the shards of life do not need to remain scattered in shame. We are new creations remade from the broken pieces of old creation.

Wounds are inevitable. Many nicks and scrapes to body or soul will resolve without incidence or even much attention. Some wounds require emergency and expert attention. All wounds leave some trauma that must be healed.

God responds to our wounds with grace because in Christ God himself has become the wounded healer. The Scriptures provide a prelude to the coming Savior not in the major key of victory but in the minor key of painful wounds. The Messiah will be *"despised and rejected by men, a man of sorrows, and acquainted with grief; and as one from whom men hide their faces he was despised, and we esteemed him not"* (Isaiah 53:3). Then, the divine strategic plan to secure victory over sin and Satan was to be wounded in apparent defeat: *"But he was pierced for our transgressions; he was crushed for our iniquities; upon him was the chastisement that brought us peace, and with his wounds we are healed"* (Isaiah 53:4).

But surely this description was just the poetic metaphor of a prophet! Actually, not. At the cross, Jesus was inflicted with wounds so incalculably terrible that only the prophetic utterance from Psalm 22 could convey the anguish that he endured, as he cried out *"My God, my God, why have you forsaken me."* Those traumatized words echo in all the wounds of humans who have sinned or been sinned against or the laments of those who have been harmed by life in a fallen world.

Even when Jesus arose victorious from the grave, those wounds left scars that testified to God's immeasurable love. To a wary and wondering Thomas who could not understand the resurrection, Jesus did not show up in transfigured glory but showed his scars, saying *"Put your finger here; see my hands. Reach out your hand and put it into my side. Stop doubting and believe"* (John 20:27). Scars became the measure of the peace-giving love of God.

Most of us will never be kintsugi artists, but all of us will need to be put back together anew and to help others to do so as well. But how? How can the shards of a life be mended? How can scars be turned into silvery slivers of redemptive beauty? Pious platitudes or well-intentioned exhortations will certainly not be sufficient and often do more harm. And while hearing a church testimony of victory or seeing the masterpiece of a life put back together may be inspiring, it can also be daunting. We can't imagine how to get there ourselves.

We need a master craftsman to take us on as apprentices. And by God's grace, we have one. I have had the privilege of knowing Colonel Steve West not only as a servant-leader in the military chaplaincy but also as a shepherd of souls—someone who has walked with men and women through the darkest valleys of trauma, grief, and loss. His ministry is not theoretical. It is forged in the crucible of real pain, real questions, and real hope.

This book is a sacred offering. It does not shy away from the rawness of trauma—the shattered identities, the silent battles, the ache of isolation, and the spiritual disorientation that often follows. But neither does it leave the reader there. He reminds us that scars are not signs of weakness but of survival—and that in Christ, even our deepest wounds can become windows of grace through which we can see God and his redemption better.

*Beyond the Scar* carries the weight of lived experience. Steve offers profound insight into the nature of trauma. He names the ache of isolation, the confusion of flashbacks, the complexity of anger, and the slow, sacred work of rebuilding trust. This is done with clinical expertise but not clinical distance. He comes along as a companion, and the book doesn't demand healing on a timeline. Instead, it offers a gentle hand and a steady voice, reminding us that healing is possible—not because we are strong, but because God is near.

If you are holding this book, it's likely because you or someone you care about has been marked by trauma. My prayer is that these pages will meet you where you are. That they will help you breathe a little deeper. That they will remind you: you are not alone. And that even the deepest scars can become signs of survival, strength, and sacred beauty.

Ultimately, this is not a book about trauma. It's a book about the hope we have in Christ. It reflects the astonishing revelation that Jesus did not leave behind the scars, but he lived beyond them. And so can we.

Walter Kim, President, National Association of Evangelicals

 PREFACE

When I first wrote *The Bronze Scar*, it wasn't meant to be a theological treatise. It was simply a raw, honest effort to help people understand how trauma—especially PTSD—feels. I wanted to give voice to the invisible wounds that many of us carry, to put words around the chaos that lives inside so many hearts and minds. That book was about empathy and awareness. It offered no real solutions; and that was intentional. Before we can begin to heal, we have to first understand what's broken. That's what *The Bronze Scar* aimed to do.

To my surprise, it found its way into college and university classrooms, used as a textbook to train future counselors, chaplains, and caregivers. That was never my original plan, but I was humbled and grateful. It confirmed what I sensed all along: people were hungry not only for explanations, but for understanding—real, human, grounded understanding of what trauma actually feels like on the inside.

But understanding alone is not enough.

That's why *Beyond the Scar* was born.

This book is not a sequel. It is a shift—from describing the wound to walking the path of healing. If *The Bronze Scar* helped name the problem, Beyond the Scar offers the solutions. Here, I invite you into a sacred process. Not a quick fix. Not a formula. But a steady, grace-filled journey toward healing—rooted deeply in a Christian worldview.

This book is written to help you walk with God through the process of restoration. It's about learning how to breathe again. To feel safe again. To trust again. It's about finding purpose on the other side of pain, and discovering that even in the middle of brokenness, Christ is near. His presence changes everything.

Every chapter includes not only psychological insights and real-life stories, but also Scriptural truth, spiritual reflection, prayer, and practices you can return to again and again. You won't just read about healing. You'll be invited to participate in it.

So if you've ever asked, "Can I really recover from this?" this book is my way of saying: Yes. And you don't have to do it alone.

Welcome to the journey—one that takes us beyond the scar, and into the arms of the Healer.

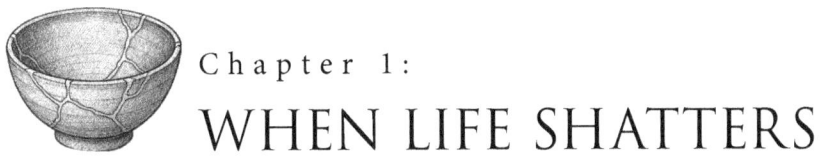

Chapter 1:

# WHEN LIFE SHATTERS

We never expect it, the phone call in the middle of the night, the sirens that blur into screams, the moment when life splits into before and after. Trauma doesn't ask permission. It arrives unannounced, uninvited, and unapologetic. One moment you're laughing at the kitchen table; the next, you're staring into an abyss of questions, disbelief, silence, and aching emptiness you never thought you'd have to face. It's not just the uncertainty—it's the searing grief of losing the life you built with your own hands, the identity you wore like a second skin, the future you spoke of without hesitation. Suddenly, what once felt certain—your calling, your family roles, your faith's footing—crumbles, and you're left holding fragments of a story you no longer recognize. The shattering leaves us suspended in a surreal in-between, where time feels both frozen and too fast, and nothing feels safe or familiar.

I've been there. And I've walked with countless others through that shattering. I remember one night, not long after a devastating personal loss, I stood outside under the open sky, too weary to pray. The stars shone above me, silent, still. And somehow, in that cold quiet, I remembered the ancient story of Abraham. God took him outside and said, *"Look toward heaven, and number the stars, if you are able to number them . . . So shall your offspring be"* (Genesis 15:5).

Abraham wasn't given answers; he was given a sky full of mystery and promise. From his vantage point, he saw only a few stars above, unable to grasp the multitude of his future descendants. All God intended for Abraham to understand was that he would have many descendants.

What strikes me most is the timing of that promise. Abraham had no children. His wife, Sarah, was barren. Everything in his present circumstances screamed the opposite of God's promise. Despite the overwhelming darkness around him, a quiet conviction filled him as he chose to believe. It wasn't rational. It was faith. He followed God's word, not his understanding. This is faith. It is the same faith we're invited to cling to when our lives break wide open and nothing makes sense anymore.

For those of us walking the long and often burdensome path of healing, our world can feel intensely confined to what is immediately visible around us. We can compare this experience to how few stars can be seen from a bustling urban backyard, obscuring the beauty of the night sky. The enormity of our pain and the deep emotional scars it leaves often act as a barrier, preventing us from fully perceiving the vast possibilities of healing that exist beyond our immediate circumstances. Just as the bright, artificial lights of a city drown out the twinkling stars, so too can the noise and chaos of life overshadow the glimmers of hope.

Yet, as we venture further into the process, stepping away from the metaphorical lights, the immediate effects of trauma, we begin to see more. Like eyes adjusting to the dark, our understanding deepens, and the path to healing becomes a little clearer. Every small revelation, each moment of support from a friend, or each successful therapy session acts like a star brightening the night sky, expanding the field of what we can see and understand. Guided by these points of light, we navigate through our recovery, much like ancient sailors who charted their courses by the stars.

Healing, like stargazing, is not about seeing everything at once but discovering what can be seen and understood a little at a time. The stars that emerge night by night in the sky are like the steps toward healing in trauma, not always visible at first glance, requiring patience and persistence to discern their patterns and meanings.

**Thus, the journey of healing unfolds not all at once, but star by star, as each step taken brings into view more of the hidden wholeness and potential of the vast human spirit.**

Just as the night sky reveals its depth only to those who learn to look beyond the glare, so too does the path of recovery slowly unveil the depth of resilience and renewal, one starlit moment at a time.

The notion of taking one step at a time is essential, especially when it comes to healing from trauma. Progress rarely follows a straight line; it meanders, with ups and downs, pauses, and strides forward. Each step, no matter how small, is a part of the journey toward healing.

Imagine walking through a dense forest. We can't see the end from where we are; the path twists and turns, obscured by trees and underbrush. But with each step, we make progress, even if it doesn't always feel that way. Some steps are small and cautious, while others are more confident and brisk. Each one is important because it gets us closer to where the trees thin, allowing in the light.

Kara was 29 when her world broke apart. Her younger brother, Josh, was killed in a sudden car accident. She got the call just after midnight. The days that followed were a blur of funeral plans, people coming by to bring food, and telling her to *"stay strong."* But strength was the last thing she felt. Nights were the worst. She'd lie awake, staring at the ceiling, her chest tight with grief, wondering if she'd ever breathe normally again.

For weeks, she functioned on autopilot. She went to work. She smiled. She said she was fine. But inside, she felt like she was unraveling. One evening, her counseling session filled with unspoken anxieties, her therapist made a surprising suggestion: step outside, find a spot where you can see the stars, feel the quiet hush of the night, and breathe deeply, letting it all go. Although it felt unnerving at first, the act became strangely familiar and comforting as she repeated it night after night.

Sometimes crying, hot, silent tears running down her cheeks, sometimes just standing still, her heart heavy with unspoken sorrow. But slowly, the fog in her mind began to clear, revealing a new perspective. The stars didn't take away her grief. But they reminded her she wasn't as alone as she felt. She began to realize her pain had a place under that vast sky. And that maybe, just maybe, there was still a flicker of hope, a fragile ember of something worth fighting for.

In this way, healing is about patience, perseverance, and acknowledging that each step, whether it feels significant or not, is moving us forward. It's about recognizing the courage it takes to make even the smallest move when everything feels overwhelming. Just as no two paths through a forest are the same, no two healing journeys are identical. Each person must find their way, step by step, at their own pace.

Don't let yourself become disheartened, for the Lord is with you in every trial. When you stand at the edge of exhaustion, grief, or fear, it can feel like God is distant—but He is not. He walks with you in the darkest valleys, even when you can't sense His presence. Every hurdle you face, no matter how overwhelming, is not just an obstacle to survive; it is an opportunity for transformation. These painful moments stretch us, refine us, and grow within us the roots of deeper faith. Trials carve out space for endurance, humility, and trust to take root. They become invitations to rely not on our own strength, but on the sufficiency of God's grace. Growth is rarely easy, and it is never instant, but it is always possible when we remain open to God's steady, sustaining presence.

*"Count it all joy, my brothers, when you meet trials of various kinds, for you know that the testing of your faith produces steadfastness. And let steadfastness have its full effect, that you may be perfect and complete, lacking in nothing"*(James 1:2-4).

Difficulties are not merely burdens to endure; they are refining fires that strengthen our spirit and deepen our dependence on Christ. When we welcome these challenges with a heart surrendered to God, we emerge not just stronger but more Christlike, bearing the fruit of perseverance and wisdom.

The way we interpret our struggles can either weaken our spirit or refine our faith. The stories we tell ourselves about these experiences can either trap us in fear and doubt or they can become testimonies of God's grace and redemptive power. So, let your trials become stepping stones toward a deeper relationship with Christ. Trust that He is working in you and through you, shaping you for a purpose far greater than you can imagine. Surrender your fears, embrace His strength, and walk forward in faith, knowing that *"He who began a good work in you will bring it to completion at the day of Jesus Christ"* (Philippians 1:6).

According to psychologists, the way we process and interpret events has a significant influence on how we handle grief or difficult experiences. For instance, if we lose someone dear to us at a young age, it can shape our belief that all our loved ones will eventually leave us. Similarly, if those taking care of us disregarded or invalidated our feelings, we may develop behaviors centered on seeking attention and approval. These encounters have the power to shake our fundamental beliefs, leading us to reevaluate and reconstruct our outlooks.

In reality, the challenges we face in life shape who we become. It's important to find meaning in our struggles and view them as opportunities for growth rather than reasons to give up hope. With perseverance and courage, we can overcome life's obstacles and emerge wiser and stronger. Though the path may not be easy, we can overcome the difficulties together if we support and encourage one another. Each challenge allows us to learn, improve, and discover new depths within ourselves. If we approach hardships with an open mind and heart, we just might surprise ourselves with that which we are capable of. The only actual failure is allowing our struggles to harden us or close us off from love. As long as we care for others and seek meaning, the light within us will never go out.

Ultimately, this process can have either positive or negative effects. It can help us thrive and find joy, or it can weaken our spirit and deepen our sense of despair. However, even if the initial meaning we gave to our experiences was unhealthy, it is never too late to create a new narrative, to rewrite the story we tell ourselves about what happened, and find healing.

Tonight, if you can, step outside. Find a quiet place. Look up. Breathe. Notice one star, or even just the darkness. Utter one honest sentence to God, even if it's just, "*I'm here.*" Let that be enough. Bring your fragments. Don't try to fix them first. Just bring them.

There are moments when life leaves a mark so deep it feels like time should stop to acknowledge it, but it doesn't. The world keeps turning, people keep living, and somehow you're expected to keep moving as if nothing has changed. But everything has. I can remember feeling like I would never again catch up with the world, like I was watching it move in fast-forward while I remained stuck in slow motion. My body went through the motions of daily life, but my soul lagged behind, weighed down by loss. There's a heartbreaking disconnection between what's happening inside and what the world expects on the outside. While your heart aches and your spirit feels splintered, life outside continues as if nothing happened.

That contrast can feel unbearable, like screaming into a crowded room where no one hears you. It's as if your pain exists in a different language that the world doesn't understand, leaving you to carry the weight alone while everything around you moves on. You wonder if anyone sees the invisible fracture lines, if anyone notices that something inside you has shifted in a way that might never fully return. It's a lonely, surreal place to be—caught between who you were, who you are now, and the aching uncertainty of who you'll become. And yet, even in that fog, God is not absent. He is present in the pause, in the in-between, gently holding space for your healing to unfold.

This book is for those who know what it's like to carry invisible wounds. It's for those who have smiled while breaking inside. For anyone who has asked, *"Will I ever feel whole again?"*—this is for you. Understand this: I acknowledge your question, your sleepless nights, your difficult mornings, and your feelings of alienation. I hear your longing. And while the answer may not come quickly or cleanly, there is a God who walks with you in the waiting, gently guiding you toward wholeness, one step at a time.

*Beyond The Scar* is not about pretending pain doesn't exist. It's about walking through it, honestly, painfully, bravely, discovering that healing is possible—even if it doesn't look the way you imagined. You don't need to have it all figured out. You don't need to be "better" already. You just need to be willing to take one honest step.

What follows isn't a formula. It's not a fix. It's a companion for the road, because healing isn't linear, and it's not quick. It's a process of learning to see the stars again when all we've known is night.

## Reflection

Healing rarely begins with clarity. It begins with presence—the quiet courage to stay where it hurts and to trust that even in the silence, God is near. We often think healing will feel like resolution, but more often, it starts with surrender. It's not about fixing everything overnight. It's about surrendering to God's presence, trusting that He doesn't wait for your wholeness before drawing near.

When we offer God our scattered pieces, He doesn't demand we glue them together first. He receives them tenderly, and in His hands, those shards begin to form something new. Maybe not what was, but something true. Something redeemed. What's broken might still bear scars, but those scars can shine with purpose and strength.

So let presence be your first step. Be where you are. Breathe. Cry. Whisper one true thing to God. That is where healing begins.

## Prayer

Father, I don't have words for all that hurts. Sometimes it feels like I've been dropped and scattered into pieces. But I believe you are near to the brokenhearted. Help me take the first step. Help me trust that You have not abandoned me. And when I cannot stand, carry me. Amen.

## Scripture

*"The Lord is near to the brokenhearted and saves the crushed in spirit."*
*Psalm 34:18*

*"Count it all joy, my brothers, when you meet trials of various kinds, for you know that the testing of your faith produces steadfastness. And let steadfastness have its full effect, that you may be perfect and complete, lacking in nothing." James 1:2-4*

*"And I am sure of this, that he who began a good work in you will bring it to completion at the day of Jesus Christ." Philippians 1:6*

## Reflection Questions

1.  When did your life feel like it shattered into "before" and "after"?

_____

_____

_____

_____

_____

2.  What lies has trauma whispered to you about your worth, your safety, or God?

_____

_____

_____

_____

_____

3. What would it mean for you to "begin again," not by fixing the past, but by stepping forward with God?

_____

_____

_____

_____

_____

4. What fragments of your life do you need to bring before the Lord today?

_____

_____

_____

_____

_____

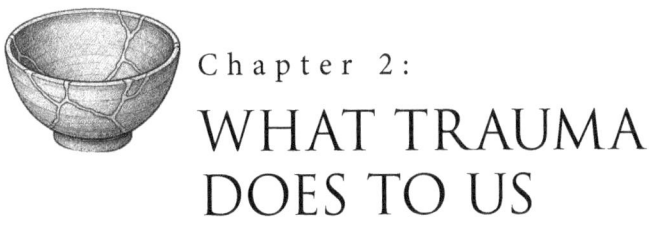

Chapter 2:

# WHAT TRAUMA DOES TO US

Trauma is not just an old wound we hide. It's a living presence. It can sit beneath the surface of our lives for years, shaping our thoughts, reactions, and relationships without our full awareness. Trauma doesn't politely stay in the past. It barges into the present and tries to dictate the future.

You can't always see it on the outside. But inside, it tightens the chest, shortens the breath, and clouds the mind. It disrupts sleep and distorts how we see ourselves and others. It makes safe moments feel dangerous, and peaceful people seem threatening. We may not remember every detail of our trauma, but our body and our soul do.

Romans 8:22–23 says, *"We know that the whole creation has been groaning as in the pains of childbirth right up to the present time . . . we ourselves, who have the firstfruits of the Spirit, groan inwardly as we wait eagerly for our adoption . . . the redemption of our bodies."* Trauma is one form of that groaning. It's a deep ache for safety, justice, and wholeness that our broken world often denies us. And yet, even in that groaning, we are not alone.

## When the Soul Feels Unsafe

It raises deep spiritual questions, often too raw to voice: *Why did God let this happen? Was He there? Does He care? Can I ever trust Him again?* These aren't just theological debates. They are cries from the deepest parts of a person. And the church has often struggled to make room for them. But scripture does.

**Trauma doesn't just leave scars on the brain; it wounds the soul.**

*"How long, O Lord? Will You forget me forever?"* (Psalm 13:1). *"Why do You hide Your face from me?"* (Psalm 88:14). These are not the words of people who have lost faith. They are the words of people who are using their faith to wrestle with pain.

Faith in the aftermath of trauma often feels like breathing through a straw. We are trying to hold on, but everything feels constricted, disconnected. Church may become difficult, not because someone doesn't believe in God anymore, but because their nervous system is still stuck in fight-or-flight, and sitting still in a pew can feel unsafe. Trauma can tint everything with suspicion—even worship. Not because the person has lost faith, but because their body no longer trusts what used to feel safe. The heart longs to sing, but the mind scans the room for exits. The soul reaches for God, but the nervous system braces for danger. In this state, even sacred spaces can feel uncertain, and the very act of worship may stir a quiet fear: *Will I break down? Will I be seen? Am I even welcome here like this?*

But the truth is, yes, you are welcome not only by those who understand trauma, but by God Himself. Scripture tells us that *"Jesus wept" (John 11:35)*. He who knew the end of the story still chose to enter into grief, to stand beside the brokenhearted, to cry with His friends. Our God is not indifferent to suffering. He does not demand polished prayers or tidy emotions. He meets us in our shattered spaces, His tears mingling with ours. When trauma makes worship feel impossible, know this: you do not weep alone, and your pain does not disqualify you from the presence of God. He is already there, waiting, grieving with you.

*"The Lord is close to the brokenhearted and saves those who are crushed in spirit"* (Psalm 34:18).

Jesus doesn't stand apart from suffering. He enters it. And in the valley of the shadow of trauma, He walks with us.

## You're Not Failing, You're Responding

One of the cruelest lies trauma tells us is that our symptoms are proof we're weak or broken beyond repair. But what if they're actually signs of how hard your body has worked to survive? Hypervigilance isn't cowardice; it's protection. Emotional numbness isn't failure; it's self-preservation. Avoidance, fatigue, even anger, they're not flaws. They're the aftershocks of something too big for your heart to hold alone.

God doesn't rebuke us for these responses. He understands them. After all, He designed our brain and body to protect us when things became unsafe. What feels like brokenness is often our body doing exactly what it was trained to do under pressure. And now, Jesus gently invites you to unlearn survival and begin relearning safety.

**Healing doesn't mean pretending the damage didn't happen.** It means learning that our present doesn't have to be ruled by our past. What looks like dysfunction may actually be evidence of our resilience, and a doorway into transformation.

Maria had always been the strong one, capable, composed, and compassionate. But after a painful betrayal by someone she trusted, something changed. Meetings made her heart race; she couldn't sit through them. She found herself snapping at her kids over little things. Afraid someone might notice her trembling, she avoided eye contact in public. Her faith, once vibrant, had dimmed. She still went to church, but the songs that once stirred her heart now sounded distant. She couldn't explain why she panicked when someone raised their voice or why she felt exhausted after small talk. She just knew something was wrong. And yet, she felt ashamed of needing help. She believed trauma was for soldiers or abuse survivors, not people like her.

It wasn't until a counselor gently said, "*You're not crazy, you're carrying pain,*" that Maria began to weep. Not out of despair, but relief. Finally, someone saw it. Her body had been telling the truth even when her mouth couldn't. Her journey of healing didn't start with a dramatic breakthrough; it started by admitting she was hurting.

## What Trauma Steals from Us

Trauma doesn't just take things away, it replaces them with something else. Rest is traded for hypervigilance. Clarity becomes confusion. Identity becomes shame. And hope? Hope gets quiet. Trauma takes more than peace of mind. It steals rest. It rewrites identity. It clouds relationships, numbs joy, and suffocates hope. It creates a gap between who we were, who we are, and who we want to be. It plants lies that sound like truth: *"You're weak." "You're broken." "You'll never be safe again."* Naming the theft is part of reclaiming what's been lost. The journey ahead isn't about going back, it's about going forward with Christ. Piece by piece, what was stolen can be restored. Safety. Trust. Clarity. Peace. Even joy. Not through denial, but through divine presence. Not by forgetting, but by rebuilding.

Healing doesn't just happen. Unlike physical wounds that sometimes heal with rest, emotional wounds resist passivity. Emotional healing requires effort. Waiting passively for trauma to resolve itself is like suffering a broken leg and refusing treatment, hoping it will straighten itself. It doesn't. Healing is hard work. It takes willpower. Motivation. Perseverance. The process is holy, but it's also labor. It may begin with asking for help, seeking wise counsel, and setting spiritual and personal goals. But it continues with practice, patience, and honest self-reflection.

Time alone won't heal a crushed spirit. Proverbs 17:22 says, *"A joyful heart is good medicine, but a crushed spirit dries up the bones."* And yet joy doesn't come without intention. Just as you wouldn't lose weight without changing habits, you won't regain your sense of safety or identity without inviting Christ and engaging your healing journey.

To heal is to fight, not against others, but for your life, your heart, and your future.

## The Power of Fear

Fear is trauma's most persistent companion. It doesn't always show up as trembling or panic. Sometimes it arrives disguised as avoidance, numbness, people-pleasing, or perfectionism. At its core, fear tells us that we are alone and we are not safe.

We're afraid of being rejected. We are afraid of being judged. We fear being misunderstood or pitied. Fear numbs us, and then it paralyzes us. The classic trauma responses, fight, flight, or freeze, aren't just metaphors. They are real neurobiological patterns. And many of us get stuck in the freeze. But fear, though it is loud, is not the Lord. *"For God gave us a spirit not of fear but of power and love and self-control"* (2 Timothy 1:7). The invitation of Jesus is not to ignore fear, but to invite Him into it. Healing is not the absence of fear; it's trusting Christ to walk with us in it.

## What if It's My Fault?

Some trauma comes from things done to us. But some come from our own choices. Regret, guilt, and self-condemnation are powerful chains. What if I hadn't gone there? What if I hadn't said that? What if I was the one who failed?

This pain is not imaginary. And God does not belittle it. But it is not the end of your story. Consider Peter, who denied Christ three times and was given three opportunities to affirm his love again (John 21). Jesus didn't erase Peter's past. He redeemed it. Romans 8:1 declares, *"There is therefore now no condemnation for those who are in Christ Jesus."* Healing includes forgiveness. It includes grace. Even if the wound was partially self-inflicted, God still brings restoration. That's who He is.

## The Weight of Invisibility

Sometimes, the greatest agony of trauma is that it hides. Many people suffer in silence, believing their pain is not valid simply because it can't be seen. A physical wound draws compassion; an emotional one often draws doubt. People don't mean to question your suffering, but when there are no visible scars, there's a quiet suspicion—like maybe you're overreacting, or maybe it wasn't that bad. But just because something is invisible doesn't mean it's imaginary. Trauma is real. Even when it leaves no mark, the eye can see.

Words can hurt worse than wounds. An insult, a betrayal, or a season of neglect can leave deep, lasting marks on the soul. Trauma is worsened when others deny it, minimize it, or spiritualize it away. *"Sticks and stones may break my bones . . . "* But trauma taught us that the rest of that phrase isn't true. Words can leave us shattered. Jesus does not dismiss your pain. He dignifies it. And He calls us into a community where invisible wounds are acknowledged, and where no one walks alone.

Looking ahead, the pages that follow are not quick fixes. They are invitations. Each chapter will focus on a dimension of healing: learning how to feel safe in your own skin again, finding a voice when silence has ruled, rebuilding trust after betrayal, forgiving when the weight is too heavy, and rediscovering joy without guilt. You'll be guided not just by insights, but by grace. By practices, Scriptures, and reflections that can be revisited again and again. This isn't a sprint. It's a pilgrimage.

If we've ever wondered whether healing is possible, this book is here to say yes, and not just in theory. Through Jesus, healing is real, personal, and sacred. Not because we forget what's happened, but because we begin to live as if redemption is stronger than ruin.

Maybe by now, you're nodding through tears. In the confusion, silence, and unanswered questions, you see your own story. We've felt it in your body, in your soul, even in your silence with God. We've been carrying something you couldn't name. Now, perhaps, you can. Remember, knowledge alone doesn't heal. This chapter has helped name the storm. The next ones will help you find the path through it. From reconnecting with your body to rebuilding trust, to reclaiming your voice and renewing your spirit, healing is possible. Not quick, not easy, but real!

This isn't a book of theories. It's a roadmap soaked in Scripture, informed by neuroscience, and grounded in grace. You are not beyond repair. You are being invited to rebuild.

## Restoring More Than What Was Lost

Jesus doesn't just return us to who we were before the pain. He makes us into something even deeper, truer, more whole. That's the promise of restoration in Scripture. In Isaiah 43:19, God says, *"Behold, I am doing a new thing; now it springs forth, do you not perceive it?"* Restoration in

Christ isn't about rewinding the tape, it's about becoming a new creation shaped by mercy, not shame.

We may carry scars, but those scars can shine with testimony. The joy that comes after trauma is different; it's not naïve or shallow. It's joy that knows sorrow and still sings. It's the miracle of resurrection playing out in slow, holy motion. And it's available to you.

## What Healing Can Look Like

Healing doesn't always feel like healing. Sometimes it looks like sitting still for five minutes without panic. Sometimes it sounds like finally saying, "*I need help.*" It might be the first time you cry in prayer, or the first time you laugh without guilt. It can mean reconnecting with your body instead of escaping it. It may begin by rebuilding trust, one relationship at a time. It can look like learning to breathe again, not just physically, but emotionally and spiritually. It might involve telling your story to someone safe. Or discovering a kind of rest you thought you'd never feel again.

It may take time. But every step is sacred. And you don't take them alone. The rest of this book will walk you through these possibilities, offering not just understanding, but practices, things you can do, pray, speak, and believe. It will help you discover that healing isn't just something that happens to other people. Christ is offering you healing, starting now.

## Reflection

Trauma rewires our sense of identity, distorts how we view the world, and tempts us to believe we are alone. But it does not have the final word.

The healing work of Christ goes deeper than the damage. His love does not rush or condemn. It walks with us, patiently restoring what was shattered. You are not broken beyond repair. You are being mended by the One who makes all things new.

## Prayer

Jesus, be near in the cracks, Jesus. You know what I've hidden and what I fear. We've seen how trauma has shaped my mind and spirit. And still, You stay. You are the One who binds wounds with kindness. You mend what the world calls broken. Be near to me in my confusion. Strengthen me to take one honest step toward healing. Let Your truth rewire fear, and Your love restore my peace. Amen.

## Scripture

*"You have kept count of my tossings; put my tears in your bottle. Are they not in your book?"* (Psalm 56:8)

*"Come to me, all who labor and are heavy laden, and I will give you rest."* (Matthew 11:28)

## Reflection Questions

1. Where in your life do you feel "stuck in survival mode"? What would it look like to feel safe again?

_____

_____

_____

2.  How do you see trauma showing up in your body or mind, through fear, forgetfulness, overthinking, emotional numbness?

_____

_____

_____

_____

_____

3.  What would your first intentional step toward healing look like? Is there someone safe you can tell?

_____

_____

_____

_____

_____

4. What do you believe God thinks about your trauma? Where does that belief come from?

_____

_____

_____

_____

_____

5. When you consider the metaphor of restoration—God mending what's been broken—what "cracks" come to mind?

_____

_____

_____

_____

_____

6. Which Scripture from this chapter stood out to you most? Why do you think that is?

_____

_____

_____

Chapter 3

# THE WAR WITHIN

Navigating the aftermath of trauma is like being stuck in a never-ending battle within ourselves. It's a constant tug-of-war between vulnerability and resilience, where one moment we may feel strong enough to face our demons, and the next we are crumbling under their weight. This internal struggle is also plagued by conflicting desires for isolation and connection, as we try to find a balance between self-preservation and reaching out for help. And then there's the constant fight between past and present, as memories and triggers pull us back into the depths of our trauma while we strive to move forward and build a new future.

For followers of Christ, this war is not just emotional or psychological, it is deeply spiritual. The Apostle Paul spoke candidly about this inner turmoil: *"For I do not do the good I want, but the evil I do not want is what I keep on doing"* (Romans 7:19). Trauma often sharpens that experience, creating an intense and confusing dissonance between who we long to be and who we fear we have become.

Yet even in this chaos, Scripture reminds us that *"the light shines in the darkness, and the darkness has not overcome it"* (John 1:5). God does not shy away from our inner war. He steps into it, bringing both comfort and clarity. Amidst this chaotic journey toward healing, there are moments of revelation, divine whispers reminding us that healing is possible. These are not mere coincidences; they are the Spirit's gentle guidance.

It's during these moments that we realize the true strength and resilience within us, gifts from a God who has not abandoned us. But even with this resilience, the road to recovery is not easy. It's filled with setbacks, doubts, and uncertainties, but also with opportunities for growth and transformation in Christ. Every scar can become a testimony. Every war-torn space in our soul can become sacred ground if we let God meet us there.

## Trauma vs. Reality

At the heart of suffering and pain, you may find yourself caught in a struggle between your past traumatic experiences and your present reality. You might often relive these traumatic events through flashbacks, nightmares, and intrusive thoughts, making it challenging to stay grounded in the now. This struggle can blur the lines between the past and present, making your body and mind react as if the trauma is still happening.

You know too well the weight of carrying your past around like an invisible backpack, heavy with memories that refuse to fade. It's as if your mind, in a desperate attempt to protect you, has inadvertently built a bridge between then and now, making you feel as though you're perpetually standing at the edge of two worlds. Every flashback, every nightmare, isn't just a memory replaying; it's an echo of your past trauma imposing itself onto your present moment, challenging your sense of safety and peace. This isn't merely the mind being overactive or the heart being too sensitive. It's a profound struggle for your sense of reality, a daily battle to remind yourself that you are here, now, and that the past doesn't have to define your present.

This echoes Paul's tension in Romans 7:9 *"I do not do the good I want, but the evil I do not want is what I keep on doing"*. The inner war of trauma is not unlike the spiritual battle between the flesh and spirit. Yet God is not alarmed by our fragmentation. He is already working toward our wholeness. *"He heals the brokenhearted and binds up their wounds"* (Psalm 147:3).

Jesus Himself experienced the weight of inner anguish. In Gethsemane, He said, *"My soul is very sorrowful, even to death"* (Matthew 26:38). He knows what it feels like to be torn by internal suffering and fear. In Christ, we are not only seen, we are understood.

These breakthroughs are fleeting at first, but over time, they anchor us. This is the sacred work of renewal, where the Spirit invites us not just to survive, but to live again.

**In moments of clarity, we begin to discern that our trauma is not our identity.**

## Safety vs. Threat

The aftermath of trauma often leaves us with a heightened sense of threat and a constant state of hypervigilance. This internal struggle revolves around the perceived need to be constantly on guard, ready to protect ourselves from harm. It's a never-ending battle between safety and threat, one that can be both exhausting and anxiety-provoking.

As one survivor shared, *"There is a level of anxiety that I can feel every moment of the day . . . that eternal internal world war."* Even King David wrote, *"I am restless in my complaint and I moan, because of the noise of the enemy . . . my heart is in anguish within me"* (Psalm 55:2-4). David's words echo the inner panic trauma survivors feel, not because danger is present, but because danger feels inevitable. The body stays on high alert, constantly scanning for threats, unable to relax. Safety becomes a distant memory, and the nervous system stays braced, as if the next blow could come at any moment. This is the torment of trauma: living in a world where the war may be over, but the soul hasn't heard the news.

And yet, David also wrote, *"When I am afraid, I put my trust in You"* (Psalm 56:3). Here lies the invitation for all of us who live in this fragile state of alertness: to hand our fear back to the One who never slumbers. Trust does not come easily to the traumatized soul, but faith gives us a place to rest while we rebuild safety in both our inner and outer worlds.

This hypervigilance is also fueled by an overwhelming sense of mistrust toward others. After experiencing trauma, it's natural to question the intentions and motives of those around us. We may struggle to trust others or form meaningful connections, as we are constantly worried about being hurt again. But Scripture gently calls us toward healing in community. *"Two are better than one . . . If either of them falls down, one can help the other up"* (Ecclesiastes 4:9-10).

Healing requires safe people and sacred spaces. It's not about pretending we're fine, but finding refuge in relationships where grace outweighs fear. Jesus Himself surrounded His ministry with people, not perfect ones, but present ones.

God never demanded we stop being afraid before we came to Him. Rather, *"Come to me, all who labor and are heavy laden, and I will give you rest"* (Matthew 11:28). In the war between safety and threat, He remains our stronghold, our shield, and our peace.

## Control vs. Helplessness

A sense of powerlessness and loss of control often characterizes traumatic events. Events beyond our control can turn our lives upside down, leaving us feeling helpless and vulnerable. This loss of control can have long-lasting effects on our mental and emotional well-being, as we struggle to regain a sense of agency in our lives.

The aftermath of a traumatic experience can be devastating. The sense of helplessness that goes with it can linger long after the immediate danger has passed. It can manifest in various ways, such as difficulty sleeping, intrusive thoughts, flashbacks, and avoidance of reminders of the event. These symptoms are often indicative of post-traumatic stress disorder (PTSD), a condition that can significantly impair a person's ability to function normally.

Beyond the psychological toll, trauma can also erode spiritual confidence. We wonder where God was in the moment we needed Him most. The stories in Scripture are full of powerless men and women who, nevertheless, found refuge in God's presence. *"The Lord will fight for you; you need only to be still"* (Exodus 14:14). This does not mean we are passive. It means we trust God's sovereignty when ours is gone.

**To heal from helplessness requires us to actively reclaim a sense of control.**

It involves recognizing that while we may not control external events, we have the power to shape our responses and reactions. As Proverbs reminds us, *"The heart of man plans his way, but the Lord establishes his steps"* (Proverbs 16:9).

Regaining a sense of control entails setting realistic goals and taking small, incremental steps. These actions reflect the Biblical principle of stewardship, faithfully managing what we can while trusting God with the rest. Cultivating self-care practices, like Sabbath rest, spiritual disciplines, and community engagement, can ground us in our identity as beloved children of God, not just victims of our trauma.

Even Jesus, facing the cross, cried out in vulnerability: *"Father, if you are willing, remove this cup from me. Nevertheless, not my will, but yours, be done"* (Luke 22:42). His surrender shows us that control is not the absence of fear, it is the presence of trust.

Scripture reassures us that God has not given us a spirit of fear, but *"of power and love and self-control"* (2 Timothy 1:7). In trauma recovery, reclaiming control isn't about mastering the world, it's about partnering with God to rebuild what was broken, one faithful step at a time.

## Isolation vs. Connection

After experiencing trauma, many people find themselves feeling disconnected, not only from others but even from themselves. The intense and complex emotions that follow trauma can make it hard to trust, to speak, or to believe that anyone could truly understand. The need for support collides with the fear of vulnerability, and this tension leads many into isolation. But what feels like safety can quickly become a prison.

God never designed us to heal alone. From the beginning, He declared, *"It is not good that the man should be alone"* (Genesis 2:18). Our need for connection is not a weakness; it is part of God's design. Isolation may feel like a shield, but in reality, it often deepens our pain.

David cried out in Psalms, *"Turn to me and be gracious to me, for I am lonely and afflicted"* (Psalm 25:16). His words echo the heart cry of trauma survivors, those who long to be seen, even while hiding. The enemy often whispers that no one would understand us, or that our pain is too much to share. But that is a lie meant to keep us in the shadows. Jesus, too, experienced loneliness. In His darkest hour in Gethsemane, He asked His closest friends to stay with Him, and they fell asleep. He knows the sting of being abandoned, and He meets us in that place with empathy, not shame.

It's true that connection takes risk. It requires the courage to let someone see the parts of us we'd rather hide. But Scripture reminds us, *"Carry each other's burdens, and in this way you will fulfill the law of Christ"* (Galatians

6:2). Our burdens don't grow lighter in isolation; they become bearable when shared.

Healing comes through community. That might look like a support group, a trusted friend, or simply one person who listens without judgment. In the body of Christ, we are not called to perfection but to presence. *"Rejoice with those who rejoice, weep with those who weep"* (Romans 12:15). That's where transformation begins, not in having all the answers, but in choosing to show up.

And when connection still feels too hard, we can begin by reconnecting with the one who understands us perfectly. *"I have called you by name, you are mine"* (Isaiah 43:1). You are not invisible. You are not forgotten. You are fully known and deeply loved by the God who sees in secret and draws near to the brokenhearted.

## Identity vs. Fragmentation

Trauma has a way of tearing at the fabric of who we are. What once felt clear, our values, our roles, our very identity, can become blurry or fractured. Many survivors describe feeling like a stranger to themselves, wondering where the person they once were has gone.

This experience of fragmentation is deeply disorienting. The pain, confusion, and fear that trauma causes can make us question not only what happened, but who we are now. And for Christians, this can become a spiritual crisis as well: *"Am I still the same person God loves? Have I become someone else entirely?"*

Scripture offers a powerful truth in the face of this despair: "*If anyone is in Christ, he is a new creation. The old has passed away; behold, the new has come*" (2 Corinthians 5:17). While trauma may distort how we see ourselves, it cannot erase who we are in God's eyes. In Him, we are anchored, even when everything else feels unstable.

Fragmentation can also stem from dissociation, moments where we feel cut off from our own experiences, as if watching life from a distance. While this can be a protective strategy during overwhelming moments, over time, it may cause deep confusion. But Jesus meets us even here. He never demanded that people be "whole" before He healed them. He embraced those whose bodies and souls were fractured.

The Gospels are full of encounters between Jesus and individuals whose identities had been overshadowed by suffering: the bleeding woman, the demon-possessed man, and the Samaritan woman at the well. Each of them came with fragmented stories, and each left seen, known, and restored. Trauma never had the last word in their lives. Neither does it in ours.

The healing journey involves reclaiming and reintegrating these lost or hidden parts of ourselves. We begin to remember that our story didn't end when the trauma happened. It's still being written, with grace, with hope, with God's restoring presence guiding us forward. As the Psalmist declares, "*The Lord is near to the brokenhearted and saves the crushed in spirit*" (Psalm 34:18).

We also find healing in naming our pain and letting trusted others bear witness to it. "*Confess your sins to one another and pray for one another, that you may be healed"* (James 5:16). This verse reminds us that community and vulnerability go hand in hand in the process of restoration.

You are not a sum of your broken pieces, nor are you less because you feel fragmented. Still, you remain a beloved image-bearer of God, held and restored day by day. What trauma has shattered, God is gently piecing back together—sometimes slowly, but always with love. *He who began a good work in you will bring it to completion at the day of Jesus Christ"* (Philippians 1:6).

## Emotional Expression vs. Numbing

One of the deepest internal battles trauma survivors face is the fight between emotional overload and emotional shutdown. On some days, you may feel like your heart is on fire, angry, afraid, or full of grief. On others, it's as if your emotions have gone silent, buried beneath a thick fog of numbness. Neither extreme is failure; both are survival responses. But neither is the destination God intends for you.

God created us as emotional beings. *"Rejoice with those who rejoice, weep with those who weep"* (Romans 12:15) is not just a relational instruction, it's a reflection of our design. Emotions are meant to be felt, named, and expressed. When trauma causes us to suppress or ignore our emotions, it interrupts our ability to connect with ourselves, others, and God.

In Scripture, we see people cry out in sorrow and sing in joy. David poured out his anguish in the Psalms. Jesus Himself wept openly at the tomb of Lazarus and groaned in the garden of Gethsemane. He did not numb His emotions; he embodied them fully, showing us that even the Son of God felt deeply and expressed it honestly.

Numbing may offer temporary relief, but it comes at a cost. It dampens not only pain but also joy, peace, and love. We cannot selectively mute emotion without dulling our capacity for hope. As Ecclesiastes reminds us, *"There is a time to weep, and a time to laugh; a time to mourn, and a time to dance"* (3:4). In Christ, healing means learning how to feel again, not all at once, but steadily and safely.

For many trauma survivors, emotional expression can be terrifying. It may feel like opening the floodgates to something too powerful to control. But emotions were never meant to be controlled like enemies. They are messengers. They tell us what hurts, what matters, and what we long for. And God meets us in those messages, not to shame us, but to guide us.

When words fail, the Spirit intercedes. *"The Spirit himself intercedes for us with groanings too deep for words"* (Romans 8:26). God is not disappointed when our prayers come as sobs or silence. He understands the language of the heart. Meredith once said, "I did not have the words for many, many, many years. This caused a lot of guilt." For so long, she believed that prayer had to be articulate to be accepted, that worship had to be spoken to be real. But God does not wait for perfect words. He hears the groanings too deep for speech, the ache behind the silence, the tear that falls without explanation. When we cannot find the words, the Spirit intercedes for us (Romans 8:26). Our silence is not a barrier—it can be a sacred offering.

It means you will no longer fear your feelings as enemies. It means you will begin to trust that your tears are safe with God and that your joy will return. You are not broken because you feel too much. And you are not failing because you feel nothing at all. Both states are places God can enter with His presence, His patience, and His promise of restoration.

**Healing from trauma does not mean you will never feel overwhelmed again.**

## Healing vs. Enduring

Many trauma survivors become masters of endurance. You get up, you function, you press on. But inside, there's a difference between surviving and truly healing. Enduring is often marked by gritting your teeth, bracing for the next impact. Healing, however, requires softness. It calls for space to feel, grieve, and be remade.

Scripture is filled with those who endured—Job, Jeremiah, Elijah, but their stories did not end with suffering. They each encountered the living God in the aftermath. Job declared, *"My ears had heard of you but now my eyes have seen you"* (Job 42:5). True healing led to a deeper relationship.

## Endurance Keeps You Alive. Healing Brings You Back To Life.

For Christians, the distinction matters. Jesus endured the cross, ". . . for the joy set before him . . ." (Hebrews 12:2). But resurrection followed. Your story, too, was made for resurrection. God does not ask you to merely survive your trauma; He invites you to be transformed by it. That transformation doesn't mean the pain never happened. It means the pain no longer owns you.

Enduring may look heroic, but healing is holy. It requires us to let God into the places sealed off. It means no longer pretending we're okay when we're not and no longer believing that suffering is more spiritual than joy. *"The joy of the Lord is your strength"* (Nehemiah 8:10).

Healing also means hope. Not toxic positivity, but the grounded, gut-level belief that God is not finished with you yet. That which broke you will not define you. That beauty can rise from ashes, not because you tried hard enough, but because grace is real.

You don't have to earn your healing. You only have to say yes to the process. Jesus never promised the healing journey would be fast or tidy, but He did promise His presence. And that changes everything. Even when you feel like you're only enduring. God is still moving. He doesn't despise your survival mode. But He longs to lead you into something deeper. Let Him. Let Him bring resurrection where we've only known ruin. Let Him teach you that healing is more than endurance. It's intimacy with the Healer Himself.

## Reflection

The war within may feel relentless, but you are not alone in it. Each internal tension, between fear and hope, numbness and feeling, isolation and connection, becomes a place where God meets you with grace. Healing is not straightforward, and it is never earned. It is a journey of returning again and again to the One who is not intimidated by your wounds. The battle may rage on, but Christ is present in the fire, whispering peace into your soul.

## Prayer

Jesus, You know the battle I'm fighting inside, the confusion, the fear, the weariness. we've walked this road of sorrow and didn't turn away. Meet me in the places I keep hidden. Give me courage to feel, to hope, and to believe again. I trust that You are not asking me to be perfect, but to be present with You. Thank You for never leaving me in the war. Lead me to peace, not just the absence of pain, but the presence of Your love. Amen.

## Scripture

"*But he said to me, 'My grace is sufficient for you, for my power is made perfect in weakness.' Therefore I will boast all the more gladly of my weaknesses, so that the power of Christ may rest upon me.*" 2 Corinthians 12:9

"*Likewise the Spirit helps us in our weakness. For we do not know what to pray for as we ought, but the Spirit himself intercedes for us with groanings too deep for words.*" Romans 8:26

## Reflection Questions

1. Which of the inner battles described in this chapter feels most familiar to you right now?

_____

_____

_____

2. What does it mean to you that Jesus understands your internal struggle?

_____

_____

_____

_____

3. When have you felt torn between enduring and truly healing?

_____

_____

_____

_____

4. How might God be inviting you to move from isolation to connection?

_____

_____

_____

_____

_____

5. What spiritual truth or Scripture from this chapter spoke most deeply to your experience?

_____

_____

_____

_____

_____

6. What might it look like to let God into one of the sealed-off places in your heart?

_____

_____

_____

_____

_____

Chapter 4:

# THE BRAIN'S EFFORTS TO HINDER HEALING

Jim said it best. *"It's like my brain's a car with the gas pedal jammed down but the brakes are barely working,"* he told me, eyes heavy with exhaustion. I knew exactly what he meant. I remember days when my head pulsed with every breath, when my mind felt like an overcharged battery, sparking and shorting out, overwhelmed, and exhausted. I'd try to quiet the storm inside, only to find thoughts swirling like smoke behind my closed eyes. That's when it hit me, trauma isn't just something that affects our emotions or our spirits. It takes up residence in the brain. It alters how we function, how we think, and how we survive.

It was only when I began learning about the brain, really understanding how it works, that the pieces of my struggle started coming together. The flashbacks, the nightmares, the hypervigilance, the dread that crept in out of nowhere weren't just emotional reactions. They were physical. They had roots in the very organ meant to help me live, think, and heal. Trauma had reshaped my brain, my command center, and that realization helped me take the first real step toward healing.

Let's get to the heart of this. When trauma hits, your brain isn't just processing it like any other memory. It's scrambling, trying to protect you. That's why it kicks into what we call survival mode. Three key players are behind the scenes: the amygdala, the prefrontal cortex, and the hippocampus. Each one has a unique role, but trauma sends them into chaos.

## Amygdala

The amygdala is like your brain's smoke alarm; it's designed to alert you to danger and keep you safe. When it senses a threat, it pulls the fire alarm and doesn't wait around for questions. It sends out distress signals, activating the fight-or-flight response. The heart races, pupils dilate, breathing quickens, and adrenaline floods the system. Cortisol comes in like the strategic general, redirecting energy to handle the crisis and etching the trauma into memory.

These hormones aren't bad. They're part of the body's God-given design to keep us alive. But when they're constantly circulating, when adrenaline is pumping in meetings, or cortisol spikes when someone knocks on the door, the brain is being told over and over, *"You're not safe."*

Over time, this rewires the brain's threat detection system. The amygdala becomes like a faulty car alarm, going off at every loud noise or sudden movement. The prefrontal cortex, which is supposed to bring logic and calm, is drowned out by the noise. The hippocampus, which should file memories into long-term storage, becomes overwhelmed and shrinks.

God created our bodies fearfully and wonderfully (Psalm 139:14), including the systems that help protect us from harm. But when trauma hijacks these systems, what was designed for our good can become a source of distress. The key is not to shame ourselves for how we feel, but to bring that confusion to the One who understands. *"Cast all your anxieties on him, because he cares for you"* (1 Peter 5:7).

The amygdala doesn't only fire when there's physical danger; it reacts when our emotional safety is threatened, too. A probing question, a certain look, or even a place can send us spiraling into defensive mode. It becomes a mental exercise in worst-case scenarios: *"What if I'm not enough?" "What if they leave?" "What if I fail?"*

**Sometimes, what's triggered isn't just fear, it's shame.**

But Scripture reminds us that perfect love casts out fear (1 John 4:18). The love of Christ is a steady presence when everything inside us screams otherwise. We are invited to come boldly to the throne of grace (Hebrews 4:16), not because we are put together, but because we are being held together.

## Prefrontal Cortex

The prefrontal cortex is the part of your brain that helps us reason, make decisions, and regulate our emotions. Think of it as the conductor of your inner orchestra. But when trauma takes over, that conductor gets drowned out by the noise of the alarm. You may try to tell yourself you're safe, but your body won't listen. The rational part of your brain is overpowered by the survival part. And so you feel stuck in this terrible tug-of-war, your mind trying to reassure you, but your body insisting otherwise.

The apostle Paul wrote about this kind of inner turmoil: *"For I do not do the good I want, but the evil I do not want is what I keep on doing"* (Romans 7:19). Trauma can heighten that internal conflict. But God does not leave us alone in the battle. Through the renewing work of Christ, we can begin to align our minds with truth, even when our bodies are struggling to catch up. *"Do not be conformed to this world, but be transformed by the renewal of your mind . . ."* (Romans 12:2).

This renewing of the mind is not a quick fix. It's the Spirit's daily work in us, healing us layer by layer. *"And we all, with unveiled face, beholding the glory of the Lord, are being transformed into the same image from one degree of glory to another"* (2 Corinthians 3:18). Such transformation takes time, patience, and grace.

Sometimes, trauma disables our ability to regulate emotionally. A word spoken without malice can feel like a dagger. A harmless situation can feel overwhelming. This is because our emotional brain, dominated by a hyperactive amygdala and a disengaged prefrontal cortex, cannot bring reason to fear. In these moments, breath, prayer, and stillness can become sacred tools. Whispering, *"Lord, have mercy,"* with slow, deep breathing is more than coping, it is worship amid chaos.

## Hippocampus

Then there's the hippocampus. This part helps you sort memories, place them in time, and make sense of what's happened. But trauma can shrink and damage it. This is why some survivors have trouble recalling events clearly, while others relive them like they're happening all over again. It's not a weakness, it's the brain struggling to process what was simply too much, too fast.

Scripture teaches us that God remembers us, even when our memories fail. *"Can a woman forget her nursing child . . .? Even these may forget, yet I will not forget you"* (Isaiah 49:15). When our minds feel broken, God's faithfulness remains intact. He holds the truth of our stories even when we cannot.

I once sat with a woman named Lily, a trauma survivor who had been living in a swirl of confusion and panic. She told me that sometimes she felt like a puppet, pulled in different directions by memories she couldn't control. When she finally saw a scan of her brain and the way trauma had lit up her amygdala, it gave her peace, not because she had an excuse, but because she had understanding. That understanding opened the door to grace. *"If this is how my brain has been surviving,"* she said, *"then I can learn to help it heal."*

Another friend, James, spent a decade in the corporate world before his trauma surfaced. He wasn't a combat veteran or first responder, he was a quiet, analytical man who'd lived through a volatile childhood. But stress at work triggered something dormant. He began forgetting important meetings. Elevators caused him to panic. He became terrified of conflict, certain any disagreement would end in abandonment. His brain had finally had enough. When he began trauma therapy, James discovered that the same mechanisms that once helped him survive were now keeping him from living. He cried when his therapist told him, *"There's nothing wrong with you. Your brain adapted. But now it's time to heal."*

Even our spiritual lives can be affected. A hyper-alert nervous system may make it difficult to feel God's presence. Some trauma survivors feel abandoned by God or fear they have done something to lose His favor. Christ, our wounded healer (Isaiah 53:5), does not draw back from our pain, He enters it. Jesus Himself experienced betrayal, abandonment, and anguish. He understands what it means to be overwhelmed in both body and soul. He is not repelled by our brokenness. He meets us in it.

Romans 8 offers us hope that healing is not only possible but promised. *"To set the mind on the flesh is death, but to set the mind on the Spirit is life and peace"* (Romans 8:6). The trauma-dominated brain often clings to survival, what Paul might call "the flesh." But life in the Spirit rewires that. It brings peace. Slowly. Gently. Through the Spirit, the brain begins to mirror what God already knows: you are safe in His hands.

In these moments, the Christian community becomes a vital source of healing. The body of Christ is meant to carry one another's burdens (Galatians 6:2), to be the tangible hands and feet of Jesus. When others sit with us in silence, pray when we cannot, or speak words of truth when our thoughts lie to us, they are taking part in our healing. No one heals alone.

The Church should be the safest place on earth for the wounded to rest. It ought to be the place where the traumatized find shelter, where the broken are not only welcomed but honored, and where the scars of past battles are met with gentle reverence. But tragically, for some survivors, the Church has not been a refuge. It has been another battlefield.

Some have been silenced in their suffering by spiritual clichés or shamed for struggling too long. Others have been retraumatized by leaders who prioritized image over integrity, or by communities that wielded Scripture as a weapon instead of a balm. When the very people who represent Christ contribute to your wound, it creates a unique kind of pain—one that cuts to the soul and distorts your view of both God and grace. This spiritual betrayal can become one of the deepest sources of trauma, leaving you questioning not just your safety, but your worth, your faith, and even your belonging in the family of God.

**Sometimes, the path to healing requires more than words. It needs embodiment.**

One powerful way to practice this is through grounding exercises combined with Scripture. For example, as you press your feet into the floor, whisper, *"The Lord is my shepherd; I shall not want"* (Psalm 23:1). As you roll your shoulders back, say, *"He makes me lie down in green pastures."* With each breath, let His Word root you in the present moment, a sacred merging of mind, body, and spirit.

We are called to be ministers of reconciliation (2 Corinthians 5:18). That includes helping others reconnect not only with God but also with themselves and their communities. When we understand trauma's effect on the brain, we become more effective instruments of healing in God's hands.

I've walked this road. I've felt like a stranger to my own mind. I've known what it is to be terrified without knowing why. Perhaps you have felt these things as well. But I've also learned this: our brains, though wounded, are still capable of healing. Neuroplasticity, that beautiful word, means the brain can change. It can grow new connections. It can learn new ways of being. It takes time, and intention, and often the help of others. But it is possible.

And the Spirit of God plays a key role in that renewal. *"He restores my soul. He leads me in paths of righteousness for his name's sake"* (Psalm 23:3). As we surrender our brokenness to Him, He begins the sacred work of restoring what trauma has tried to steal.

Healing is both spiritual and physiological. The God who knit us together in our mother's womb (Psalm 139:13) is more than able to reweave the frayed cords of our minds. And He often does so through community, therapy, prayer, and time. *"He heals the brokenhearted and binds up their wounds"* (Psalm 147:3).

The key is compassion, both for yourself and for others who've been through trauma. Healing doesn't come from just "thinking differently" or "pushing through." It comes from understanding what's really going on beneath the surface, and then gently, patiently working to calm the alarm, restore balance, and rebuild trust in your own mind again.

So, if you're reading this and your brain feels like it's at war with yourself, I want you to know— you're not broken. You're human. We've endured more than most people will ever understand. And even in the middle of the chaos, you're already doing something incredible; you're seeking healing. And that is the beginning of everything.

The healing journey is often not a linear process. Some days will feel like breakthroughs, while others will feel like setbacks. But every moment spent seeking peace is valuable. Even your tears are sacred to God. *"You have kept count of my tossings; put my tears in your bottle"* (Psalm 56:8). Every faltering prayer, every small act of self-kindness, every effort to reach out for help, it matters. It all adds up. God wastes nothing in your story. Not your pain, not your questions, not your waiting. He is present in every part of it.

## Reflection

Your trauma changed your brain, but it didn't destroy your ability to heal. In fact, recognizing what's happening neurologically can be one of the most empowering steps you can take. You're not weak for struggling. You're strong for surviving. And you're wise for wanting to understand.

## Prayer

Lord, You are the Creator of our minds and the Healer of our hearts. When my brain feels broken, remind me that You are still holding me together. Teach me to trust the healing process, to be patient with myself, and to believe change is possible. Calm my fears. Quiet the alarms. Guide me gently into peace. Amen.

## Scripture

*"Do not be conformed to this world, but be transformed by the renewal of your mind..."* (Romans 12:2)

## Reflection Questions

1. When have you felt like your brain was working against you? What helped in that moment?

   _____

   _____

   _____

   _____

2. Can you recognize when your body goes into "survival mode"? What are your signs?

   _____

   _____

   _____

   _____

3. Which of the brain's three parts, the amygdala, the prefrontal cortex, or the hippocampus, feels most affected in your experience?

_____

_____

_____

_____

_____

4. How might understanding the brain's response to trauma help you be gentler with yourself?

_____

_____

_____

_____

_____

5. What spiritual practices help you feel grounded and safe when anxiety or fear rises?

_____

_____

_____

_____

_____

6. Who is someone in your life who understands your journey, and how can you invite them into your healing process more intentionally?

_____

_____

_____

_____

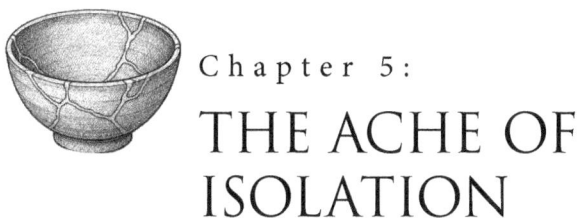

Chapter 5:

# THE ACHE OF ISOLATION

To walk through trauma is to carry an ache that isn't always visible but weighs heavily on the soul. Among the deepest wounds trauma inflicts is the feeling of isolation, being physically present yet emotionally distant, surrounded by people yet feeling completely alone. For many trauma survivors, isolation doesn't begin with a conscious choice. It begins with exhaustion, overstimulation, and a profound sense that the world no longer feels safe or understandable.

Trauma can make the whole world feel unsafe, and even people we love can become sources of fear. When hypervigilance sets in, our nervous system can't differentiate between real danger and imagined threat. So we pull back, not because we want to, but because our brains are screaming for silence. We pull away from others as a way of surviving what our brains have decided is still a battlefield, even if we are safe now. The nervous system remembers.

And yet, in Scripture, we see God stepping into isolation. Elijah, hiding in a cave, believed he was the last faithful man alive. He cried out, overwhelmed and alone. But God met him there, not in fire or earthquake, but in a gentle whisper. God's presence did not erase Elijah's fear. It reminded him he was not abandoned.

One of the deepest spiritual wounds of trauma is not just the loss of safety, but the loss of connection—connection to God, to others, and even to ourselves. This disconnection, if left untreated, can fester into bitterness or spiritual numbness. David, in the Psalms, often cried out in anguish, asking, *"How long, O Lord? Will you forget me forever?"* (Psalm 13:1). This cry reflects a soul that feels abandoned, even by God.

## Pulling Away Without Meaning To

In my own journey, I never wanted to be alone. I loved being with people. I avoided eating alone, going to the movies alone, or even sitting in public spaces alone. But trauma reversed that. When I began to suffer its effects, I found myself pulling away from others. My wife noticed first. I needed more time alone, and large crowds or deep conversations became too taxing.

It wasn't that I stopped loving people. It was that being around them made my anxiety rise. My brain, on constant alert, couldn't handle the stimulation. I wasn't retreating to avoid others; I was retreating to survive.

Sometimes we don't even realize we've withdrawn until the loneliness sets in. We decline invitations without knowing why. We make ourselves too busy for social interactions. We watch from a distance as life moves on without us, unsure how to rejoin it. And the longer we stay disconnected, the harder it is to believe reconnection is possible.

One person told me, *"I used to love going to church, sitting in the second row, and hugging every person who walked in. Now, just the thought of walking through the lobby gives me chest pain."* That's what trauma does. It shrinks our world until joy feels out of reach.

The ache of isolation crept in quietly. Sometimes it was as simple as not answering the phone. Other times it was choosing the back pew of the church and slipping out early. It was the disconnection that comes when you are physically present but emotionally unreachable.

## The Double-Edged Sword of Solitude

Solitude can be healing. Jesus Himself withdrew to lonely places to pray. Sometimes trauma survivors need quiet to process what's happened and to regulate their overwhelmed nervous system. But left unchecked, that need for solitude can spiral into full-blown isolation, and isolation can become dangerous.

Some solitude is sacred. But prolonged isolation is not holiness, it's a form of hiding. It can reinforce the lie that no one will understand or care about you. That lie keeps us in the dark. Solitude becomes isolation when it's no longer healing, but numbing. When silence is no longer restful but suffocating. When the presence of others no longer feels like a possibility, but a threat.

It's one thing to say, *"I need time alone to heal."* It's another to say, *"I don't want anyone near me because they can't possibly understand."* The latter is a lie trauma often tells us, that we are too broken to be loved, too complicated to be helped.

A trauma victim once told me, *"It's not that I don't want to be with my family. It's just that I don't know how anymore."* That's what trauma does, it doesn't just change what happened. It changes what we think is possible.

God's grace, however, invites us out of hiding. Jesus didn't just call people to come and follow, He went to where they were. He broke bread with outcasts, sat with the grieving, and embraced the leper before he was clean. God's response to our isolation is not judgment. It is pursuit.

## When Others Don't Understand

There's a unique pain that comes when others pull away because they don't understand what you're going through. Maybe your moods have changed. Maybe your energy is unpredictable. Maybe your words are harsh because your soul feels raw. To the outside world, you may seem angry, distant, or difficult. But inside, you're just trying to survive.

People who haven't walked the trauma road can't always see that. They don't realize you're fighting to stay afloat—that every day takes energy just to function, to show up, to keep going. They don't understand that silence might be the only safe space you have left. That your absence doesn't mean you don't care—it means you're overwhelmed. They misread your retreat as disinterest when in truth, you're doing everything you can to keep from falling apart. The very things that help you survive—pulling back, going quiet, guarding your heart—can be mistaken as coldness or pride. And so, on top of the pain you already carry, you're left with the grief of being misunderstood.

This can compound your pain. Now you're not only suffering from the trauma itself, you're grieving the

**The ache of loneliness is not just because people are gone, but because even the ones who stay don't always know how to reach you.**

loss of connection, the fear that you're too much for others to handle. You want closeness, but you fear being misunderstood. That tension becomes its own kind of trauma. Sometimes, others leave not because of our brokenness, but because they don't want to face their own. Our trauma is a mirror, and not everyone wants to look into it.

Isolation grows when misunderstanding meets silence. And too often, shame keeps us from correcting the misinterpretation. Instead of saying, *"I'm struggling,"* we say nothing. And silence becomes our language. When others leave, it hurts. But when we leave ourselves, when we abandon the parts of us that long for relationship, for safety, for peace, that's a deeper pain still. It is the ache of believing we no longer belong anywhere.

## Empathy as the Antidote

Empathy is one of the greatest gifts a trauma survivor can receive. When someone chooses to stay, even when they don't understand, when they say, *"I'm not going anywhere, even if you can't talk"*, that act of presence begins to mend what isolation has broken.

Empathy says, *"You don't have to explain everything. I just want to be with you."* That kind of love breaks through the walls we build around ourselves. It doesn't demand performance or productivity. It simply offers presence. *"Rejoice with those who rejoice, weep with those who weep"* (Romans 12:15). Empathy is showing up without needing to fix anything.

When someone stays long enough to hear your silence, something holy happens. Empathy brings light to places that have only known shadows. It reminds us we are not invisible. We are not too much. We are not alone. A friend who listens with compassion may not change your circumstances, but they will change your sense of worth. Presence is powerful medicine. In moments of empathy, we catch glimpses of the character of Christ, who did not just preach sermons but touched the unclean, knelt with the grieving, and wept with His friends.

## Trauma's Impact on Connection

When we experience trauma, especially chronic trauma, it changes our relational wiring. The amygdala, constantly scanning for threats, can make even small misunderstandings feel like major betrayals. The prefrontal cortex, which helps us regulate emotional responses and maintain perspective, often becomes less active. This makes emotional regulation and clear communication difficult. Our nervous system becomes dysregulated, and it takes less and less to trigger a fight, flight, or freeze response. In such a state, even well-meaning interactions can feel like emotional ambushes. The natural response is to retreat.

Sometimes the sound of a phone ringing can feel like too much. A knock at the door triggers panic. Invitations to "just come hang out" are declined, not because we don't want to, but because the idea feels overwhelming.

Even touch, which should feel safe, can startle us. Kindness feels foreign. We second-guess compliments. The brain tries to protect us from anything it can't predict. And since connection involves unpredictability, it often feels dangerous. But in doing so, we miss out on the very thing we need most: connection. Loneliness becomes familiar. We adapt to the ache. But deep down, we know we were made for more.

God did not create us for isolation. From the beginning, He said, *"It is not good that the man should be alone"* (Genesis 2:18). He created us for connection: deep, honest, vulnerable relationships. Healing means learning how to move toward what we were created for, even when everything inside us screams to withdraw.

## The Internal War

There's a war that takes place inside many trauma survivors, a war between wanting to be close to others and needing to protect themselves. It's not about inconsistency or moodiness; it's about survival. One minute, closeness feels comforting; the next, it feels like a trap. This internal conflict makes relationships difficult and adds yet another layer of isolation. We retreat not because we don't love others but because we don't know how to stay present when our insides are on fire. We push people away not because we want to, but because we're terrified of hurting them, or being hurt.

We build emotional walls, not to imprison ourselves, but to keep pain out. But walls block the light, too. Healing begins when we allow those walls to become windows, when we let God's light and the compassion of others shine in. Understanding this war within is crucial to achieving peace with ourselves and cultivating healthy, healing relationships. It allows us to name our behaviors not as failures but as adaptations. With that clarity comes grace. Grace says, "You did what you needed to survive." But healing invites us to learn how to live.

## Kintsugi and the Beauty of Reconnection

The art of Kintsugi teaches us that broken things can be made beautiful again, not in spite of the cracks, but because of them. God doesn't discard the shattered parts of our lives. He pieces them back together with grace, creating something more valuable, more resilient, and more beautiful than what existed before.

In *The Bronze Scar*, I described chaplaincy as showing up for people in places where their souls had cracked wide open, such as hospital rooms, battlefield tents, and prison cells. These were sacred spaces, not because they were perfect, but because truth and presence met there. That's what reconnection looks like after trauma.

Reconnecting after trauma isn't about pretending you're okay. It's about slowly and tenderly rebuilding trust—trust in yourself, in others, and in God. This is about finding people who will sit in the silence, love without making demands, and who will see your pain and not turn away. It means learning how to open your heart again. To accept love when it's offered.

To believe truth even when it feels distant. To welcome safe touch without fear. To embrace grace without shame. Reconnection is holy work. It is a spiritual discipline. It is the slow weaving of soul back into soul. And this reconnection is not just with people—it's with your calling, your creativity, your sense of wonder. It's with laughter, with nature, with prayer, with music. All the things trauma tried to erase, God gently restores.

## The Courage to Re-Engage

Choosing to come out of isolation takes courage. It means risking misunderstanding. It means being vulnerable when you'd rather be safe. But it's also the only way to truly heal. Connection is a risk, but it's one worth taking. Start small. Reach out. Let someone in. Say, *"I'm not okay, but I'd like to try."*

God's invitation has always been toward community. Toward communion. Toward belonging. He who made Adam said it was not good for man to be alone. Jesus surrounded Himself with friends, even knowing they would misunderstand Him. He returned to them, even after they failed Him.

Paul reminds us that the Church is one body with many members. No single part of the body can say to another, *"I don't need you"* (1 Corinthians 12:21). In healing, we rediscover our place in that body. We learn to receive again. To trust. To hope.

Let Kintsugi remind you: the cracks are where the light gets in. And as the golden seams of connection begin to form again, you may find that the ache of isolation slowly gives way to the warmth of presence. You are not too much. Nothing about you is too broken to be mended. Loneliness does not define your story. And even now, the long work of reconnection is already underway.

## Building Bridges One Step at a Time

Reconnection doesn't happen overnight. It begins with simple, often unnoticed steps: making eye contact with a neighbor, texting a friend back, showing up to a small group even when you'd rather stay home. These small acts are not insignificant; they are bricks in the bridge we are building back to others.

Healing is rarely loud. It whispers in quiet choices: choosing compassion over self-judgment, extending forgiveness even when we're still hurting, allowing someone to pray for us when we don't have the words ourselves. Each choice to engage, however small, is a declaration that trauma will not have the final word. Sometimes the bravest thing you can do is to say "yes" to an invitation. Not because you feel ready, but because you believe healing is worth the risk. Courage doesn't always roar. Sometimes it whispers, *"I'll try again tomorrow."*

## Letting God Reframe the Story

Scriptures are filled with stories of isolation being met with divine presence. Joseph was abandoned by his brothers and imprisoned, yet God was with him. Hagar ran into the desert, and God found her. Jesus Himself withdrew to lonely places, not to escape, but to commune with the Father.

*"Fear not, for I have redeemed you; I have called you by name, you are mine. When you pass through the waters, I will be with you"* (Isaiah 43:1-2). He does not shame us for needing solitude. He blesses the quiet places. But He also gently nudges us back into community, reminding us that the Body of Christ is a lifeline, not a luxury. You don't have to fix yourself to belong. You already do.

> **God doesn't wait for us to be healed before He meets us. He steps into the ache with us.**

Healing from isolation begins with a willingness to believe that new connections are possible, that God can send new friends, restore old ones, and sustain us even when we feel unseen. The story isn't over. The ache will not last forever. And the God who calls us His own is already at work weaving your life back into something beautiful.

This is not the end of your story.

## Reflection

This chapter explored how trauma can lead us into isolation, physically, emotionally, spiritually, and how even in that place of loneliness, God meets us. We examined how trauma affects our relationships, our ability to trust, and our longing to reconnect. We were reminded that isolation is not the end of the story, and that healing often begins with small, intentional steps toward reconnection.

Reflect on how these themes resonate with your own experience. What stood out to you? What new insight did you gain about the ache of isolation and the courage it takes to re-engage?

## Prayer

Heavenly Father, when my heart retreats and my spirit feels hidden, draw near. Remind me that I am never truly alone. Meet me in my isolation with Your gentle presence. Help me to see Your hand in the quiet, Your love in the stillness, and Your grace in every attempt to reconnect. Teach me to trust again, myself, others, and most of all, You. Thank You for never abandoning me, even when I pull away. Rebuild my life with golden seams of mercy. In Jesus' name, Amen.

## Scripture

*"Fear not, for I have redeemed you; I have called you by name, you are mine. When you pass through the waters, I will be with you"* (Isaiah 43:1-2).

## Reflection Questions

1. What are some signs that you may be retreating into unhealthy isolation?

2. Who in your life has shown up for you in a way that brought healing?

_____

_____

_____

_____

3. What is one step you could take this week to move gently back toward connection?

_____

_____

_____

_____

4. How has trauma changed your understanding of God's presence in your solitude?

_____

_____

_____

_____

5.  How can the image of Kintsugi help you reframe the scars left by isolation?

Chapter 6:

# THE WEIGHT OF ANGER AND THE BATTLE TO FORGIVE

Anger is one of the most misunderstood responses to trauma. It rises like a wave; unpredictable, sharp, and often frightening to those around us and even to ourselves. But anger is not inherently wrong. In fact, it can be one of the most honest emotions we feel after being hurt. It tells us something important: a boundary has been violated, something sacred has been lost, and we are in pain.

For trauma survivors, anger is rarely simple. It's often layered beneath sorrow, fear, or grief. And when left unprocessed, it can morph into bitterness or self-contempt. But when held with compassion and brought into the presence of God, anger can become a doorway to healing.

## When Anger Speaks the Loudest

Anger after trauma is typically not triggered by a single incident. It's the echo of a hundred moments when we weren't heard, protected, or believed. It's the voice that says, *"This should not have happened."* When trauma is ignored or minimized, anger becomes the protector. The part of us that refuses to let the pain be buried again.

Some people learned early in life that anger was dangerous. Maybe it led to violence or was punished instead of understood. So we pushed it down, only for it to resurface later as anxiety, depression, or chronic tension. Others were taught in church that anger is a sin, forgetting that Scripture says, *"Be angry and do not sin"""* (Ephesians 4:26).

Jesus Himself expressed anger-righteous anger. He overturned tables in the temple when God's house was being exploited (Matthew 21:12-13). He wept with those who mourned, confronted hypocrisy, and grieved over injustice. His anger was not destructive. It was purposeful. It was rooted in love.

## What Lies Beneath the Surface

Anger is often a secondary emotion. Beneath it, there's usually something more tender: sadness, fear, shame, or loss. When we only deal with the anger, we miss the deeper wound. But when we dare to ask, *"What's underneath this rage?"* we start to heal from the inside out.

**Unacknowledged grief fuels many of our sharpest outbursts.** The unspoken sorrow of what was taken from us, our innocence, our trust, our safety, demands a voice. And sometimes, anger is the only way we know how to express it.

Naming that grief doesn't weaken us. It frees us. As we learn to name the pain behind the rage, we begin to feel less hijacked by it. We begin to respond, not just react.

Anger that is silenced often festers. But when we make space for it, we learn that it is not a threat. It is a messenger. It tells the truth about our pain. And truth, even when it burns, is the beginning of transformation.

## The Brain's Role in Our Anger

Trauma shapes the brain. It rewires the nervous system to remain in a state of high alert. The amygdala becomes hyperactive, constantly scanning for threats. The prefrontal cortex, which plays a crucial role in reasoning and regulation, becomes overwhelmed. This is why trauma survivors often describe going from zero to sixty in an instant. The brain isn't malfunctioning. It's protecting.

But healing is possible. Practices such as deep breathing, grounding, and somatic prayer can help soothe the nervous system. And as the body finds safety again, the brain starts to recalibrate. Anger becomes less about survival and more about healing.

**We must remember anger is often a biological response before it's a moral one.**

The shame we feel over our anger is often misplaced. What our bodies need is not more self-rebuke, but gentleness and retraining. We are not bad because we feel angry. We are wounded. And wounded people need care, not condemnation.

## The Role of the Church in Healing or Harming Anger

For some, the church has been a place of deep healing. For others, it has been a source of dismissal or even deeper wounding. When anger is labeled as unspiritual, or when expressions of hurt are met with clichés instead of compassion, survivors can begin to believe that God, too, rejects their pain. Some are told to "*forgive and move on*" without any room for lament, honesty, or acknowledgment of the offense.

But the Gospel is not afraid of anger. The God who calls us to be slow to anger also modeled what it means to be angry for the right reasons, in the right way, and with a heart still open to redemption.

We must create space within our faith communities for the full range of human emotion. Church should be the place where the angry find rest, not rebuke; where lament is welcomed, not silenced. As leaders, pastors, and friends, we must be brave enough to sit with people in the heat of their emotions without rushing them toward resolution.

## The Invitation to Slow Healing

There is no fast track to healing anger. It takes time. Often, more time than we want to give it. But God's pace is not rushed. The same God who formed the world in six days has no problem walking slowly beside a broken heart for as many years as needed. He is not disappointed by the fact that you're still angry. He knows what it's rooted in. And he is endlessly patient.

So, take your time. It circles back to hurts you thought were over. That's not a sign of failure. That's how deep wounds heal.

**Healing is not a straight path. It loops. It revisits old places.**

Sometimes, the anger resurfaces after long stretches of calm. That doesn't mean we've failed in our healing. It means we've encountered another layer that needs tending. Each return of anger is an invitation to pause, to listen, to bring it again to the One who knows us intimately.

## A New Relationship with Anger

Eventually, the goal is not to eradicate anger, but to make peace with it. To recognize its presence without being consumed by it. To use it as a mirror, not a weapon. To ask: What is this anger trying to tell me about where I still need healing, where I still feel unseen, where I need boundaries, where I need God?

Anger, in this renewed sense, becomes less of a threat and more of a companion on the healing journey, a voice that demands to be heard, but one that can be responded to with kindness, with Scripture, with truth, and with grace.

## Forgiveness Revisited

One of the most helpful distinctions for trauma survivors is the difference between forgiveness and reconciliation. Forgiveness is a one-person decision. It's an inner posture, a surrender to God's justice. Reconciliation, on the other hand, requires repentance and change from the offender, and it may never be safe or appropriate. Forgiveness: It's possible to forgive someone while still maintaining boundaries. You can forgive and still press charges. You can forgive and never see them again.

It's worth repeating: forgiveness is not a magic trick or a forced smile. It is not a declaration that all is well. It is the decision to entrust justice to God, and to refuse to let the offense own any more of our future. It's a practice, not a performance. And it is always, always empowered by grace.

The same grace that makes room for your anger also makes room for your freedom. You can hold both. And one day, maybe not today, you will be able to say, *"That wound no longer defines me."* This is what forgiveness makes possible. And when you get there, it will not be because you forced yourself. It will be because God walked you gently, faithfully, and patiently through every step.

## The Connection Between Anger and Identity

Anger is often tied to the places where we feel unseen, misunderstood, or undervalued. When someone questions our integrity, ignores our pain, or betrays our trust, it touches something deeper than the immediate offense; it stirs the question of who we are and whether we matter. That's why the wounds tied to identity can carry the most enduring anger. We're not just reacting to the hurt; we're reacting to the violation of our very sense of self.

This is why healing from anger is also a work of identity restoration. We remember that we are not defined by what happened to us or by how others have treated us. We are defined by the One who calls us beloved, who knit us together with intention, who meets us in the fury and says, *"Even this is not too much for Me."*

God is not threatened by our anger. He invites it. He holds it. He redeems it. And in doing so, He restores what was lost-not just our peace, but our sense of who we are.

## A Story of Wrestling and Release

Lena carried her anger like a stone in her chest. It had been there for years, long after the abuse, long after the courtroom, long after the apologies that never came. It didn't erupt daily, but it lived in her, tightening her voice, pulling her shoulders in, shadowing her joy. She didn't want to be angry. She just couldn't seem to shake it.

In counseling, she once said, *"I know I'm supposed to forgive. But every time I think I've gotten there, something happens-a word, a memory, a dream-and I'm back in that place again. It's like my heart has scar tissue that keeps tearing."*

But week by week, her therapist helped her name the anger without rushing to fix it. They read Psalm 55 together-David's cry of betrayal by a close friend: *"For it is not an enemy who taunts me-then I could bear it . . . But it is you, a man, my equal, my companion, my familiar friend."* In those verses, Lena finally felt understood. Her rage was not just grief. It was grief over broken intimacy. Over love weaponized over safety shattered.

As Lena learned to grieve the relationship she had hoped for, not the one that had been, her anger began to shift. It didn't vanish, but it softened. It lost its sharpness. What remained was sorrow, holy sorrow, and a strange kind of strength.

Forgiveness came not as a final verdict, but as a rhythm. Some days, she had to choose it again. Other days, she simply held it loosely, trusting that God would carry what she could not.

## Divine Justice and Human Surrender

One of the most challenging aspects of anger is the desire for justice. We want the wrongdoer to feel the weight of what they've done. We want fairness. And God does too. Scripture tells us that justice matters to Him deeply. *"For the Lord is a God of justice; blessed are all those who wait for him"* (Isaiah 30:18).

But justice in God's hands looks different than revenge in ours. It is redemptive, not destructive. It seeks restoration, not just retribution. When we entrust justice to Him, we are not saying the offense was small. We are saying His hands are big enough to hold it.

That doesn't mean we never take action. Sometimes justice means confronting, reporting, and setting boundaries. But it also means we don't have to carry the weight of being judge and jury. We can rest, knowing that nothing escapes God's sight and nothing is beyond His redemption.

## One More Story: Micah's Turning Point

Micah had grown up in a home where feelings weren't just dismissed—they were punished. Anger was met with silence or scorn. So he learned to keep his rage bottled up, only for it to erupt later in ways that shocked even him. As an adult, he struggled with chronic frustration and shame. He snapped at his kids, shut down during conflict, and often found himself apologizing for things he couldn't quite explain.

In one particularly raw session with his pastor, Micah confessed, *"I'm not even mad at my wife half the time. I think I'm just still yelling at people who aren't even in the room anymore."*

That moment became a turning point. Together, they explored what it might look like to bring those decades-old wounds into the light. Micah began journaling his memories—writing letters he never sent. He practiced speaking his truth aloud in prayer, trusting that God could handle the intensity. And over time, the volume of his rage began to quiet. Not because he denied it, but because he finally let it speak.

## Jesus and the Holy Tension

When we wrestle with anger, we're not alone. Jesus, in His humanity, felt it too. He wept at Lazarus' tomb not just from grief, but from frustration over death's grip on creation. He cried out in anguish at Gethsemane, not to escape pain, but to express it fully before the Father. And in the temple, His anger at injustice was not wild—it was purposeful. *"Zeal for your house will consume me"* (John 2:17).

Jesus shows us that holy anger exists: anger aligned with love, grounded in justice, fueled by compassion. He never harmed in rage. But He never silenced truth to avoid conflict either. If Jesus could feel anger without sin, then maybe our goal isn't to eliminate it, but to redeem it. Let prayer, instead of despair, be our guide. To fuel protection, not retaliation. To awaken justice, not vengeance.

## Practices That Makes Room for Healing

What do we do when anger rises in daily life—when we can't escape it and don't want it to consume us? We start with presence. Not performance. Not suppression. Presence.

- **Name it.** Say aloud: *"I am angry."* It sounds simple, but it moves the emotion from reaction to awareness.

- **Locate it.** Where is it in your body? The clenched jaw? The pounding heart? Noticing it helps you anchor.

- **Ask it.** What is this anger trying to protect? What pain is underneath?

- **Invite God.** Speak honestly. Even if your prayer is just one line: *"Lord, I don't want this anger to rule me."*

- **Move gently.** Go for a walk. Breathe slowly. Cry without judgment. These are not small acts—they are sacred ones.

None of these fixes the deeper wound overnight. But they create space for God to meet us in the middle of it. And with time, that space becomes a sanctuary—not where anger is forbidden, but where it is heard, healed, and eventually transformed.

## An Invitation to Breathe

If all of this feels overwhelming, start here: take a deep breath. Let yourself be right where you are. No timeline. No pressure. Just breathe. Inhale the truth that God is near. Exhale the lie that healing must be hurried.

The same Jesus who wept at a friend's tomb and who sweated blood in Gethsemane, understands. He welcomes the ache, the tension, the tears. You are not too much. Your story isn't too complex for Him. Your anger is not disqualifying. It is the place where grace wants to begin.

## Reflection

This chapter explored the way anger functions in the aftermath of trauma, not as weakness, but as a sign of deeper wounds. We looked at how sadness often hides beneath the rage, how trauma shapes the brain's response, and how anger, when honored and brought to God, can become a pathway to healing. Forgiveness, then, is not the erasure of pain but the transformation of it, made possible only through compassion and grace.

## Prayer

Lord, You see my anger. You know the grief beneath it, the injustice behind it, the wounds it tries to protect. Help me to stop running from it and to begin listening to it. Teach me to bring it to You, not in shame, but in hope. Transform this fire into light. Help me release what no longer serves me, and trust You with the justice I can't carry. Make me whole again. In Jesus' name, Amen.

## Scripture

"*Be angry and do not sin; do not let the sun go down on your anger.*" (Ephesians 4:26)

"*In all their affliction he was afflicted...in his love and in his pity he redeemed them.*" (Isaiah 63:9)

"*Know this, my beloved brothers: let every person be quick to hear, slow to speak, slow to anger; for the anger of man does not produce the righteousness of God.*" (James 1:19-20)

## Reflection Questions

1. What situations or relationships tend to trigger your anger most often?

---

---

---

---

---

2.  What emotions might be hiding underneath that anger?

_____

_____

_____

_____

_____

3.  How can you begin to offer grace to yourself in the moments when anger flares?

_____

_____

_____

_____

_____

4.  What practices help you move from reaction to reflection?

_____

_____

_____

_____

_____

5. What would it look like to let God use your anger, not to destroy, but to heal?

_____

_____

_____

_____

_____

Chapter 7:

# THE GRIEF TRAUMA LEAVES BEHIND

A scent, a sound, a glance, these ordinary things can become powerful reminders of our deepest pain. For those living with trauma, such "triggers" are not just unpleasant memories. They can launch the mind and body back into the very moment of suffering, bypassing logic, prayer, or preparation. It's as if the soul shatters all over again.

For many trauma survivors, flashbacks are the most disorienting experience of all. One moment they're standing in the grocery store, and the next, their body tenses, heart races, and brain is flooded with past fear. These are not "imaginary." They're real responses, rooted in the brain's survival wiring. And when these moments hit, they can cause even the strongest believer to question their healing, their faith, and their future.

## What Are Triggers?

Triggers are any stimulus—internal or external—that causes a traumatic memory to resurface, often with the same intensity and emotion as the original event. Triggers can be visual (a person's face), auditory (a song, a sudden bang), olfactory (the smell of a hospital), or even emotional (feeling powerless, lonely, or unseen).

Many trauma survivors live on high alert, always scanning the environment for potential threats. This hypervigilance is not a lack of faith—it's a survival strategy the brain adopted to stay alive. The amygdala, the brain's fear center, often hijacks the rational parts of the brain, such as the prefrontal cortex, when a trigger is detected.

Some triggers are obvious. Others sneak up in ways you'd never expect. For me, it's the sound of a car door slamming. It's such a small, everyday moment—mundane for most people. But for me, it carries the weight of memory.

When my wife gets out of the car and shuts her door a little too firmly, the sound doesn't just register in my ears—it reverberates through my chest. Modern vehicles are sealed so tightly that a door slamming causes a kind of pressure wave inside the cabin. That sudden shift of air, that deep thud of impact, does something inside me. It unsettles something buried.

Without warning, I'm no longer in the car, I'm back in uniform, crouched low, heart racing. The noise echoes the rush of moments when I had to hit the ground fast. There was no ceremony to it, no grace. It was a reflex wired by survival. Drop now, think later. And underneath that motion was always a silent question: Is this it? Will I get back up this time?

Even though I'm safe now, my body remembers. Trauma has a way of imprinting on the senses, so that something as simple as a sound becomes a doorway to the past. It's not about logic. It's about what your nervous system learned under fire—and how long it can take to unlearn it.

For Christians, this experience can be confusing. You might believe we've forgiven, let go, or moved on—only to be ambushed by emotional intensity you didn't expect. The reality is, healing is not a straight line. Triggers don't mean we've failed. They mean you're still healing. *"He heals the brokenhearted and binds up their wounds"* (Psalm 147:3).

## Understanding Flashbacks

These aren't just memories; they are immersive, sensory experiences that can make it difficult to distinguish past from present. Some experience dissociation— feeling emotionally or physically detached—while others become overwhelmed with terror or shame.

**Flashbacks are moments when a person feels as though they are reliving a traumatic event.**

Kayla, a combat medic, once shared: *"I was at a 4th of July picnic, and when the fireworks started, I hit the ground before I even knew what I was doing. Everyone stared. I felt humiliated. But my body wasn't being dramatic. It was protecting me."*

Kayla's reaction is not rare. Trauma changes how the brain stores memory. Instead of being filed away in the past, traumatic memories can live in the present tense. The brain treats them as unfinished business, especially if healing has been incomplete.

Flashbacks can include physical symptoms: nausea, cold sweats, dissociation, trembling, crying, or going numb. The body often "remembers" trauma long before the conscious mind understands what's happening. *"My soul is cast down within me; therefore I remember you"* (Psalm 42:6).

## The Nervous System and Trauma

One way to understand trauma responses is through the lens of the autonomic nervous system, especially the polyvagal theory. This theory explains how our bodies automatically shift between states of calm (ventral vagal), fight-or-flight (sympathetic), and freeze/shutdown (dorsal vagal) depending on how safe or threatened we feel.

Triggers activate the sympathetic system, flooding the body with adrenaline and cortisol. When that doesn't resolve the perceived threat, some people drop into the freeze response. In these moments, someone may feel paralyzed, numb, or emotionally checked out. Knowing this doesn't solve trauma, but it provides language and understanding. You are not crazy. You are not spiritually defective. Your body is trying to protect you with the tools it has.

## Learning to Live With Triggers

Healing from flashbacks and triggers requires time, patience, and grace—especially grace toward oneself. Some hope that spiritual maturity or time alone will erase these moments. But in truth, deep healing often happens not in spite of these moments, but through them.

## Name the Trigger

Instead of running from what you're feeling, name it. "*This is a flashback.*" "*This is a trauma response.*" Naming what's happening separates you from the fear. You are not your trauma.

## Ground in the Present

Use grounding techniques: press your feet into the floor, describe five things you see, or touch a textured object. These simple acts help pull your nervous system out of panic and into the present.

## Breathe with Purpose

Deep breathing engages the parasympathetic nervous system. Try breath prayers: inhale, "*Lord Jesus,*" exhale, "*have mercy on me.*"

## Practice Compassion, Not Condemnation

God is not disappointed in your flashbacks. He is close to the brokenhearted (Psalm 34:18). Trauma is not sin. Your responses are not rebellion. They are human.

## Seek Safe Community

Trusted friends, pastors, or support groups can remind us of truth when our brains are drowning in lies. "*Therefore, encourage one another and build one another up*" (1 Thessalonians 5:11).

## Create a Safety Plan

Having a plan in place for when triggers strike can give back a sense of control. This might include calling a trusted friend, retreating to a safe space, or engaging in a spiritual ritual that grounds you in God's presence.

Sometimes, the greatest healing begins when we stop trying to "fix" ourselves and start allowing ourselves to be cared for by God, by safe people, and by the grace woven into every breath.

## Grieving What Was Lost

Sometimes, the most profound grief doesn't come from death, but from the life we were never given. Dreams that withered unspoken. A childhood lost before it began. Safety that was always out of reach. These quiet losses often go unnoticed by others, but they leave deep wounds, nonetheless. And they, too, are worthy of grief.

You may find yourself mourning things you can't quite put into words: the way you used to laugh without flinching, the belief that people could be trusted, the ease with which you once occupied your own body. These are not small losses. They are sacred. And they matter to God.

**Grief in the aftermath of trauma is not simple.** It's cyclical, sometimes confusing, and always holy when brought into God's presence. Some days you may feel light and hopeful, only to be plunged back into sorrow the next day. Healing doesn't mean the grief disappears. It means you learn how to carry it with grace.

When Jesus said, *"Blessed are those who mourn, for they shall be comforted"* (Matthew 5:4). He was talking to people like us—those who have mourned not just the loss of others, but the loss of ourselves.

God does not rush that process. He doesn't scold us for crying again. He doesn't roll His eyes when the same sorrow resurfaces. Instead, He holds space for our tears. He collects them. *"You have kept count of my tossings; put my tears in your bottle. Are they not in your book?"* (Psalm 56:8)

## Community and the Witness of Compassion

Trauma isolates. Grief compounds that isolation. But healing rarely happens in solitude. It grows in the soil of a safe connection. The presence of another person—someone who listens without fixing, sits without preaching, sees you without judgment—can be the difference between feeling like a burden and knowing you are beloved.

You may have been wounded in a relationship, but relationships are also where God does some of His most powerful healing. A friend's text message at just the right time. A mentor who shares their own scars. A support group where you don't have to explain why you flinch when someone raises their voice. These moments stitch your story back together with threads of grace.

The Church, when it's at its best, becomes that sanctuary. Not a place of performance or perfection, but a refuge for the weary and the wounded. In community, the lies of shame begin to break. The story that said, "*You're too much,*" gets rewritten as, "*You are deeply known and still deeply loved.*"

And when someone else opens up their pain to you, it becomes sacred ground. Their story, too, bears the image of God. Their grief echoes your own. And together, your presence becomes a kind of liturgy—a shared declaration that trauma does not have the last word.

## Redeeming the Wreckage

We don't get to erase the past. And healing doesn't always mean understanding why the trauma happened. But the Christian story tells us that God redeems what others meant for harm. He rebuilds what was shattered. Not always the same as before, but often stronger, richer, and more deeply rooted in grace.

Your story isn't too messy for redemption. God doesn't edit out the hard parts. He weaves them into something breathtaking. And that doesn't mean you have to smile through your sorrow or pretend you're grateful for the pain. It simply means that your pain is not wasted. God wastes nothing.

Even your flashbacks—those unwanted revisits to the past—can become invitations to deeper healing. They show you where your soul still aches, where your heart still needs tending. And when you invite Jesus into those moments, you may find Him not distant, but near, closer than your next breath.

The cracks in your life are not signs of failure. They're places where the light can get in. Kintsugi, the Japanese art of repairing broken pottery with gold, reminds us that the mended places can become the most beautiful. Your story, too, can shine with the brilliance of redemption—not in spite of your pain, but because of it.

## Embodied Grace: Worship in the Aftermath

Grief and trauma can feel like they fracture us; mind over here, body over there, soul somewhere in between. But God made us whole beings, and the work of healing includes bringing all of who we are back into alignment. Worship is not just singing. It's presence. And sometimes, the most sacred worship is allowing yourself to feel again; to cry, to tremble, to laugh, to rest.

Worship is also an act of resistance. When you worship through your pain, you are declaring that trauma does not own the final word. When you raise your voice in praise, however shaky or soft, you are reminding your soul of its eternal anchor. Worship becomes a bridge between sorrow and hope, reminding us that even when we feel far from God, He is never far from us.

For some, worship may take the form of singing old hymns that evoke a sense of childhood safety. For others, it may be sitting in silence with tears streaming down their face while a worship playlist plays in the background. There is no formula. What matters is the turning of the heart toward the One who sees you fully and loves you completely.

The Psalms are a gift for this kind of worship. They permit us to say it all; the anger, the fear, the doubt, and the praise. They teach us that lament is a form of faith. That questioning does not disqualify belief. And that God can handle every emotion we bring before Him.

Each time you breathe deeply and remind your body that it is safe, you are participating in resurrection. Each time you let someone in instead of pushing them away, you are reclaiming sacred ground. Each time you name your grief and lift it to God, you are practicing resurrection hope. The world says healing is self-made, self-driven, and self-earned. But the Gospel says healing comes from grace, and grace is always a gift.

So if today all you did was survive, that is still holy. If all you could offer was a whisper of a prayer, God heard it. If the only thing you managed was staying present, even for a moment, heaven rejoices. Healing doesn't begin with heroic acts. It begins with quiet surrender to the God who weeps with you, walks with you, and never leaves your side.

The valley of the shadow does not have the final say. The Shepherd is with you there, preparing a table in the presence of your fear. And one day, even this grief—raw and unwelcome as it is—will be redeemed. Not erased, but transformed. And you, beloved, will bear the beauty of one who has walked through the fire and come out gold-laced.

## Reflection

Grief is the quiet companion of trauma. It walks beside us, often unnoticed, until we turn and acknowledge its presence. This chapter is an invitation to do just that. To mourn what trauma took from you. To stop minimizing your losses. To believe that your grief matters to God. There is healing in that naming. There is grace in that sorrow. And there is Jesus, acquainted with grief, walking with you in yours.

## Prayer

Lord, I bring You the grief I've tried to bury. The sorrow I was told to get over. The losses that still ache within me. Thank You for being a God who sees, a Savior who weeps, and a Comforter who stays. Teach me to lament. Help me identify my losses and trust you to restore what is possible. Meet me in this grief with tenderness and truth. In Jesus' name, Amen.

## Scripture

*"Blessed are those who mourn, for they shall be comforted."* Matthew 5:4

*"You have kept count of my tossings; put my tears in your bottle."* Psalm 56:8

## Reflection Questions

1. What are some specific losses we've experienced as a result of trauma that we've never named aloud?

_____

_____

_____

_____

2. How have shame and grief overlapped in your story? What would it look like to separate them?

_____

_____

_____

_____

3. Who are the safe people in your life who can walk with you in your healing journey?

_____

_____

_____

_____

4. What would it mean for you to believe that God meets you in your trauma, not after we've healed, but in the very middle of it?

_____

_____

_____

_____

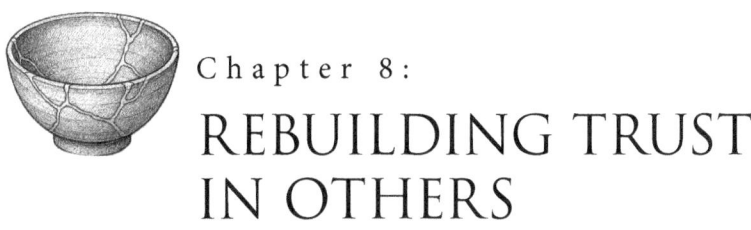

Chapter 8:

# REBUILDING TRUST IN OTHERS

Trust is one of the first casualties of trauma. Whether the trauma came from violence, betrayal, abandonment, or systemic harm, the ability to believe others are safe, and we ourselves are safe, can be deeply fractured. For many survivors, rebuilding trust feels like learning to walk again after a devastating fall. It's slow, painful, and full of uncertainty.

Broken trust is hard to rebuild, and it shouldn't be easy. Rebuilding trust after trauma is tender, slow work. Whether it's trust in others, in God, or in ourselves, the road back can feel uncertain and fragile. Trust doesn't come easily when it's been broken, and it shouldn't. In this chapter, we'll walk gently through what trust really is, why it feels so elusive after wounding, and how it can begin to grow again. Not in rushed or perfect ways, but in ways that honor your story, your boundaries, and the God who is patient with both. Along the way, Scripture, psychology, lived experience, and grace will help light the path forward, one small step at a time.

Trauma dismantles our sense of safety. What once felt predictable or secure becomes threatening. We learn to flinch at kindness, brace for disappointment, or retreat from connection. Whether the trauma came from a person, a system, or even our own bodies turning against us, trust is one of the deepest losses we endure. And trust is not just external.

**Rebuilding trust must start within, but that is often the hardest place to begin.**

Many survivors stop trusting their own instincts, bodies, or decisions. *"How did I not see it coming? Why didn't I say no? Why did I go back?"* These questions aren't just self-reflection, they're indictments we quietly carry.

Trust is not blind optimism. It's not pretending nothing happened. It is an act of courage. It is saying, *"Even though I've been hurt, I believe healing is possible. I believe people can still be safe. I believe God is still good."* But that belief doesn't come all at once. It begins with small, sacred steps.

Rebuilding trust with others requires discernment, patience, and a willingness to start small. For someone who has been hurt by a loved one or betrayed by someone in authority, the idea of trusting again can feel impossible. It's not just fear, it's wisdom born of pain. And yet, isolation can never fully heal what was wounded by connection—whether it was a relationship, a community, a church, or a place that was meant to be safe. What was damaged in relationships is often only restored through connection, slowly and gently, in spaces where trust can grow again.

We heal in relationships. A safe, consistent, respectful connection is one of the strongest antidotes to trauma. That doesn't mean we throw ourselves into risky dynamics or offer trust indiscriminately. Rebuilding trust is not about being naïve, it's about recognizing when someone has earned your vulnerability and giving it gradually, intentionally.

Look for people who show up, not just speak up. Those who honor your boundaries, who apologize when they're wrong, who listen without trying to fix or minimize. These are the bricks in the new foundation of safety. And remember: trust doesn't mean perfection. It means knowing someone is trying. It means they value you.

Daniel was a man who had been deeply betrayed by a leader he trusted. The wound left him wary not just of authority, but of people in general. He was isolated, spiritually disconnected, and doubted his own judgment. When he finally began counseling, he was hesitant to share. But week by week, through quiet presence and honest reflection, trust began to rebuild, not just in his therapist, but in himself as well.

Daniel once told me, *"I thought trusting again meant being naive. But now I see that trust is actually the bravest thing I've ever done."* His story reminds us: trust can be lost, but it can also be rebuilt, layer by layer, step by step.

Trust can be lost in a single instant. That's what makes it so devastating. A single lie, a moment of betrayal, or a broken promise can shatter what took years to build. One glance, one choice, silence at the wrong time, and suddenly, the foundation that made us feel safe is gone. It's not just painful, it's disorienting.

Many survivors of trauma will tell you that few things wound more deeply than being intentionally misled. When someone lies to us, not just to cover a mistake, but with calculated intent, it cuts differently. It breaks something sacred. Because trust isn't just about behavior, it's about belief. It's the belief that someone sees you, respects you, and will protect what matters to you. When that is violated, we don't just question the other person, we begin to question everything: our judgment, our worth, even our reality.

You may forgive. You may even reconcile. But trust? That takes time, sometimes months, sometimes years. Sometimes, it never returns to what it was before. And that is a hard truth to face.

Sometimes we forgive because we are commanded to. We choose grace. We choose release. But forgiveness does not reset the clock on trust. Even after the words *"I forgive you"* have been spoken, a lingering wariness often remains. Sometimes we stay in the relationship, but something shifts. Caution replaces ease. The benefit of the doubt fades. We start scanning for tone, noticing inconsistencies, bracing for the next letdown. Some may call it cynicism, but for many of us, it's not about bitterness. It's survival—learned through pain, practiced through experience.

This doesn't mean we're bitter. It means we're healing. When someone earns back trust through repeated honesty, accountability, and humility, relationships can be restored, but they're never exactly what they were. Sometimes they're stronger. Other times, they settle into a different shape. Still valuable, but changed.

Almost everyone who has experienced betrayal will say this: *"I can forgive. But I will never forget how that moment changed me."* And that's not bitterness, it's reality. It's what helps us draw wiser boundaries and love with open eyes. It's what helps us show up more honestly for ourselves.

So, if you feel like you're still guarded, even after we've forgiven, know this: you're not wrong. You're not weak. You're being wise. And wisdom, when mixed with grace, is what makes new trust possible.

You're not where you were. And you may not be where you once hoped to be. But you are still moving forward. And that matters. A lie. A betrayal. A broken promise. It takes only one moment to dismantle what may have taken years to build. And when that moment comes, the damage ripples out, shaking not just the relationship but the survivor's ability to feel secure anywhere.

One of the most consistent truths I've heard from trauma survivors is this: few things hurt more than being intentionally deceived. Whether it's a spouse, a friend, a spiritual leader, or a parent, when trust is broken, it alters how we see the world. Even when forgiveness is offered, the effects of that betrayal linger. You can forgive someone, but it doesn't automatically restore the relationship to what it once was. In some cases, it never returns. In others, it can be rebuilt, but slowly, and never without scars.

Trust is not guaranteed simply because we choose to forgive. It must be earned again through consistency, honesty, and humility. And even then, most people who have been betrayed will tell you that while they may resume a relationship, they do

**Forgiveness is a command, but reconciliation is a process.**

so cautiously. They are more alert. More guarded. More discerning. And that's not unspiritual, it's wise.

Learning to live again after broken trust means accepting that some relationships may change permanently. It also means understanding that your guardedness is not weakness; it's a signal that your heart is trying to heal. With time, wisdom, and God's grace, you may discover new levels of trust, perhaps not as naive, but more rooted, more resilient, and more real.

Rebuilding trust doesn't mean everything gets tied up neatly. It means learning to live with tension: believing God is good while still grieving what happened. Loving others while guarding your boundaries. Believing in your voice while still having moments of doubt. This is not spiritual failure; it's sacred recovery.

Jesus didn't promise we wouldn't be wounded. But He did promise His presence. He said, *"In the world you will have tribulation. But take heart; I have overcome the world"* (John 16:33). To trust again after trauma is to risk again. To hope again. And that hope is holy.

For many survivors, trauma shakes the foundation of their faith. The God they once trusted now feels silent or distant. They ask hard questions: *Where was God? Why did He let this happen? Can I trust Him again?*

These questions aren't a sign of weak faith, they are the beginning of a deeper, more honest relationship with God. He is not offended by our doubts or our pain. In fact, Scripture is full of lament. The Psalms cry out, *"How long, O Lord? Will you forget me forever?"* (Psalm 13:1). Jesus

Himself cried, *"My God, my God, why have you forsaken me?"* (Matthew 27:46).

Rebuilding trust in God starts not with answers but with presence. When we stop pretending and begin praying from the raw places, something sacred happens. God meets us in the honesty. He doesn't demand polished prayers. He asks for real ones.

Faith after trauma isn't about returning to the way things were. It's about discovering that even in the wreckage, God is still with us. His faithfulness doesn't erase our pain, but it promises we won't walk through it alone.

Perhaps the most fragile thread to restore is the one that connects you to yourself. Trauma doesn't just make us wary of others or doubtful of God, it teaches us to mistrust our own instincts. You may question your memories, your choices, and your voice. You may look back and wonder, *"Why did I freeze? Why didn't I speak up? Why did I go back?"* These aren't just questions; they're often accusations we silently hurl at ourselves.

But here's the truth: you survived the best way you could at the time. What may look like failure or passivity now was likely your nervous system doing what it was designed to do: protect you. The freeze response isn't a weakness. Dissociation isn't cowardice. These are survival strategies. And they worked. You are here.

Rebuilding trust in yourself begins with compassion. Not denial, not rationalization, but the tender, intentional choice to see yourself through the eyes of grace. You don't have to earn self-trust with perfection. You rebuild it with presence. One moment at a time.

Trusting yourself also means listening to your body again. After trauma, your body may have become a source of distress. But healing comes when you begin to notice its cues, not as threats, but as signals. Hunger, exhaustion, tears, tension, these aren't betrayals; they are your body speaking. And you get to listen with kindness.

You are not your worst day. You are not the moment you froze. You are not the voice that went silent. You are resilient. And your ability to trust yourself again is already unfolding, one step at a time. Healing requires more than distance from the past. It calls us to be accountable and present, both to ourselves and to others, and to the God who walks with us through the work of restoration. That kind of trust isn't found overnight, but when it's found, it's sacred.

## Reflection

This chapter explored the delicate, courageous journey of rebuilding trust, trust in others, in God, and in ourselves. Trauma doesn't just break our sense of safety; it undermines the very foundation of connection. But healing is possible. Trust can be restored slowly, faithfully, and with grace. Whether it's trusting someone new, daring to believe God is still near, or learning to befriend your own body again, every step matters.

## Prayer

God, you know the wounds that have made it hard for me to trust. You see the parts of me that still flinch, still fear, still retreat. I ask for your healing touch on every broken place. Help me to trust again, not blindly, but bravely. Teach me to discern what is safe and to walk with wisdom. Be my refuge when the world feels unsteady, and be my strength when I want to shut down. Thank you for never giving up on me. Amen.

## Scripture

"*Trust in the Lord with all your heart, and do not lean on your own understanding. In all your ways acknowledge Him, and He will make straight your paths.*" Proverbs 3:5-6

"*In the world you will have tribulation. But take heart; I have overcome the world.*" John 16:33

"*How long, O Lord? Will you forget me forever?*" Psalm 13:1

## Reflection Questions

1.  In what ways has trauma affected your ability to trust others, God, or yourself?

_____

_____

_____

_____

_____

2. Who in your life has shown safe and consistent presence?

_____

_____

_____

_____

_____

3. What would rebuilding trust with yourself look like in small daily actions?

_____

_____

_____

_____

_____

4. What boundaries or practices could support healthy trust going forward?

_____

_____

_____

_____

5. What step, however small, can you take this week to move toward trust?

_____

_____

_____

_____

_____

Chapter 9:

# FINDING PURPOSE AFTER PAIN

Pain has a way of making us feel like our lives have been reduced to ashes. When we walk through trauma, we often lose not only our sense of safety and stability, but also our sense of direction. The dreams we once had, the roles we once cherished, the meaning we once found, they can all feel suddenly distant or destroyed. Purpose feels impossible when we're just trying to survive.

Still, something sacred happens in the ruins. God is not only present in our pain, He is at work in it. Scripture shows us again and again that out of suffering, new strength can rise. *"To give them a beautiful headdress instead of ashes, the oil of gladness instead of mourning, the garment of praise instead of a faint spirit"* (Isaiah 61:3). He does not waste our wounds. He reshapes them.

Think about what it means to find purpose after pain. How does trauma reshape our identity? How does God connect with us in hardship? How can we transform even our most painful experiences into something meaningful? This isn't about ignoring that trauma was bad; it's about understanding that even what was meant for evil can be transformed into something good (Genesis 50:20). Finding purpose after pain isn't a one-time revelation; it's a lifelong process of rediscovery, restoration, and hope. Let's walk that road together.

Trauma has a way of disconnecting us from the stories we were writing. Maybe you were building a career, nurturing a family, serving in ministry, or pursuing a dream. Then something happened—an assault, a loss, a betrayal, a tragedy—and everything changed. What once gave you a sense of meaning now feels inaccessible. You may even feel foolish for having believed in it so deeply.

Purpose isn't just about what we do; it's about how we see ourselves. Trauma often distorts that vision in subtle but devastating ways. It doesn't just disrupt our plans; it rewrites the narrative of who we are. We begin to believe lies like, "I'm broken beyond repair," or "Nothing I do will matter now." These aren't passing discouragements, they become core assumptions that affect how we show up in the world. They disorient our internal compass and make the thought of purpose feel unreachable.

These false beliefs can become so deeply ingrained that even moments of hope feel suspect. You may hear encouragement from a friend or sense a spark of interest in something again, only to immediately push it down: *"Why bother? I'll just fail."* But here's the truth: those lies aren't the end of your story. They are the fog. And even though it's hard to see through, the road is still beneath your feet. You're still on it. The fact that you're reading this now, still seeking, still wondering, means you haven't given up. And that is purpose, too.

But purpose is never truly lost; it's often buried beneath the rubble of grief and fear. Sometimes we have to excavate it. Other times, we have to allow something entirely new to emerge. Healing doesn't always mean returning to what was; it sometimes means stepping into what could be. And that future, however uncertain, can still be beautiful.

There's a strange paradox in suffering: the very thing that wounds us can also wake us. It brings a rawness to life, stripping away illusions and distractions and forcing us to confront what is real. Many people who endure trauma discover **Pain can sharpen our awareness of what matters most.** a depth of insight, compassion, and clarity they never knew they had. It deepens empathy, stretches our spiritual imagination, and creates a hunger for justice and healing, not just for ourselves, but for others.

This doesn't justify what happened. God grieves with us in our suffering. But it does reveal what God can do in its aftermath. Out of ashes, He can grow beauty. Out of brokenness, He can shape strength. And out of the deep silence of suffering, He can call forth a voice that carries healing for someone else still lost in the dark.

Pain strips away pretense. It exposes what matters. It can reveal a calling you never would have considered otherwise. Many counselors, chaplains, pastors, and advocates entered their vocations not because life was easy, but because their own pain became a bridge to someone else's healing.

In *The Bronze Scar*, I wrote about how PTSD reshaped my ministry. It didn't make me less effective, it made me more human. I stopped trying to fix people and started sitting with them. I began to see purpose not just in preaching from a pulpit, but in offering presence, honesty, and solidarity. That shift didn't erase my pain, but it gave it direction.

One lie Satan whispers most often in our brokenness is this: *"You can't be effective anymore. we've been disqualified."* That deception plays perfectly into his plan, to shift our focus off of what God can do through us and instead fixate us on what we can't do ourselves. It's a subtle distortion that breeds self-doubt and paralyzes us from pursuing our calling. But that's a lie born from shame, not from grace.

The simple truth is this: God is always with us. And thankfully, it doesn't depend as much on us as it does on His power working in us. The distinction is subtle, but vital. Satan wants us to focus on us—on our limits, our wounds, our shortcomings. But the strength doesn't come from us. It comes from Christ in us. *"I can do all things through him who strengthens me"* (*Philippians 4:13*). The key is not in the 'I can,' but in the 'through Him.'

Our effectiveness in God's Kingdom does not rely on being unbroken— it relies on being available, being real, and being willing to let God redeem even the hardest parts of our story. Our scars don't make us unusable. They make us relatable. They become the places where *"God's power is made perfect in weakness"* (*2 Corinthians 12:9*).

You don't have to turn your trauma into a platform. But you do have a story. And your story carries weight—not because it's perfect, but because it's real. Someone needs what we've learned. Someone is waiting for the kind of grace you now carry.

One of the most liberating shifts in healing is realizing that purpose doesn't have to look like it used to. Before trauma, we may have had big visions, platforms, careers, and goals clearly mapped out. After trauma, our capacity may look different. Our passions may shift. What once felt central may now feel out of reach or unimportant. And that's okay.

Purpose isn't always about the spotlight. Sometimes it's about being present for your grandchildren. Sometimes it's about walking beside a friend who's grieving. Sometimes it's about returning to church after a long absence and choosing to worship through tears.

God never measures our purpose by productivity. He measures it by faithfulness. The world might overlook the quiet courage it takes to face each day, but God sees it. He honors it. And He calls it good.

Redefining purpose means giving ourselves permission to value what matters now, not just what mattered then. It means recognizing that your impact may come through consistency, compassion, or quiet wisdom. Purpose doesn't have to be grand to be Godly. It just has to be rooted in love.

An essential part of how we are made is our deep need to live with purpose. Purpose grounds us, motivates us, and gives direction to both our healing and our hope. We are wired to believe our lives matter. And in many ways, it is in our scars that we learn the most about ourselves, and often find the greatest capacity to help others who are hurting.

Brandon pastors a church whose motto is "Living Life on Purpose." That simple phrase says so much. It reminds us that purpose isn't reserved for moments of strength, it's something we can carry into every moment of our lives, including the broken ones. Finding purpose wherever we are, especially in the aftermath of pain, is what helps us move forward. It is what lifts our heads, steadies our feet, and invites us to believe our story still matters.

Even when it feels like everything has unraveled, God is still at work weaving purpose into the fibers of your story. It's like looking at the back of a beautiful piece of needlework; threads crossing in complete disorder, colors tangled, and patterns impossible to follow. From that side, it looks like chaos. It's hard to keep track of where anything begins or ends. That's often how our lives feel in the midst of trauma: messy, jumbled, and unfinished.

But flip the embroidery over, and suddenly, the image is clear. The artist's design comes into view—purposeful and beautiful. That's what God sees. While we may only see the tangled side of the tapestry, He is creating something meaningful on the other side. The beauty is already there—it's just not always visible from our perspective.

This is how God sees us: not as tangled threads, but as a masterpiece in progress. And it's how He longs for us to see ourselves. Even in our pain—even in the chaos of life's processes and decisions—He sees beauty. He may not take all the chaos or pain away, but He wants us to trust that beauty exists above and beyond it. Wouldn't it be wonderful if we could see ourselves the way He does? To look into the mirror and see not just the scars and the shattered plans, but the strength and sacredness God is shaping within us? What He sees is not damaged goods but deeply beloved children. He sees a story still unfolding. A vessel not discarded, but one being refined. A purpose not lost, but emerging, thread by thread.

Even when we can't see clearly, when all we recognize is the tangled mess beneath, God invites us to trust the process. The full design is visible to Him. With every choice, every tear, each act of courage and whispered prayer, He is stitching something purposeful and beautiful. What feels chaotic to us is part of a pattern He already knows. That is the beauty He wants us to believe in, not someday, but now. Because this beauty is not separate from our suffering, it is woven into the tapestry of our healing. Every thread, even the dark and tangled ones, is part of what God is redeeming. This isn't just a metaphor about life—it's about trauma, pain, and the toll they've taken on us. It's about learning to see even the broken pieces of our story as places where healing is being stitched in by a loving hand.

When we talk about finding purpose after pain, we're not suggesting we forget what happened or pretend it didn't leave scars. We're saying that in the very process of recovery, in the hard decisions, the grief, the rebuilding, purpose is taking form. And God is inviting us to see the emerging picture through His eyes: not as victims of chaos, but as beloved participants in redemption. What if we could look beyond the mess and catch a glimpse of the glory He's weaving through every thread?

Sometimes we don't catch a glimpse of that picture until much later, when someone says, *"Your words helped me,"* or "Because of you, I didn't give up." That's when we begin to realize that even our pain has been carrying purpose. *"And we know that for those who love God all things work together for good, for those who are called according to His purpose"* (*Romans 8:28*). It doesn't say all things are good. But it does promise that God can work in all things. That includes your story. That includes your trauma.

In the hands of God, nothing is wasted. Every scar, every sleepless night, every broken prayer—He sees it all. And He is faithful to turn even the ashes into something sacred. Sometimes, that sacred work looks like a renewed calling. Sometimes, it looks like comfort offered to someone else. And sometimes, it simply looks like survival with grace. Purpose isn't always loud. Sometimes it's the quiet conviction that your life still matters—and that your healing will ripple into the world in ways you may never fully see.

## Reflection

We were reminded by this chapter that pain did not destroy that purpose; it was often refined by it. Your trauma may have interrupted the path you were on, but it did not erase the meaning of your life. God is not finished with your story. In fact, He may be just beginning a new chapter. As you heal, your life becomes a light, quiet, steady, and holy.

## Prayer

Lord, when I look at the broken pieces of my life, it's hard to see purpose. I confess that some days I feel lost, aimless, or empty. But I believe You are still writing my story. I believe You can take what the enemy meant for evil and redeem it. Show me, step by step, how to live with meaning again. Help me trust that even my smallest acts of courage carry purpose in Your hands. Amen.

## Scripture

*"To grant to those who mourn in Zion—to give them a beautiful headdress instead of ashes, the oil of gladness instead of mourning, the garment of praise instead of a faint spirit." Isaiah 61:3*

"You meant evil against me, but God meant it for good." Genesis 50:20

*"The Lord will fulfill his purpose for me; Your steadfast love, O Lord, endures forever." Psalm 138:8*

## Reflection Questions

1. How has trauma impacted your understanding of purpose?

_____

_____

_____

_____

_____

2. What small acts of healing or faithfulness have carried new meaning for you?

_____

_____

_____

_____

_____

3. Are there ways we've seen God use your pain to help others?

_____

_____

_____

_____

_____

4. What fears or doubts make it hard to believe your life still has meaning?

_____

_____

_____

_____

_____

5. What one step could you take this week to move toward purpose, no matter how small?

_____

_____

_____

_____

_____

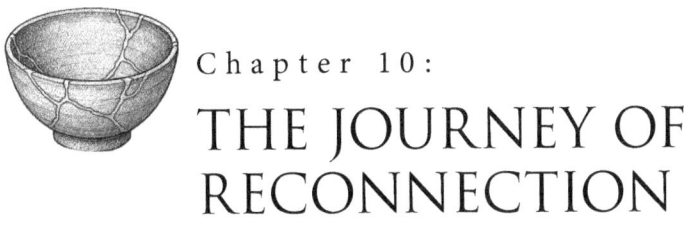

Chapter 10:

# THE JOURNEY OF RECONNECTION

Trauma doesn't just wound our minds or bodies, it fractures our sense of connection. Connection to others. Connection to ourselves. Connection to God. It isolates, divides, and casts long shadows over the parts of life that once felt safe and familiar.

What is the journey of reconnection? It's about discovering, one step at a time, that while trauma may have severed certain bonds, healing can reweave them, sometimes in new and unexpected ways. Reconnection is not about returning to how things used to be. It's about discovering a new kind of closeness, rooted in authenticity, courage, and grace.

Before we ever seek reconnection, we have to name the ache of disconnection. One of the cruelest lies trauma tells us is that no one else could possibly understand our pain. It convinces us that we are safer alone. And for a time, solitude can feel like a sanctuary, quiet, predictable, and under control. But left unchecked, that protective silence hardens into a wall that keeps others out and locks our hearts. We become like cities with gates closed to even the kindest visitors. We nod and smile, but inside we feel miles away.

This isolation isn't always a conscious choice. Often, it begins as an autonomic nervous system response to chronic stress and trauma. The body remembers, even when the mind wants to move on. Hypervigilance sets in, and our systems remain on high alert, constantly scanning for threats. When everything feels overwhelming, withdrawal feels like a matter of survival. But surviving isn't the same as living. We may breathe, eat, work, and function, but connection, purpose, and peace remain just out of reach.

In that place, the enemy often whispers another lie: our brokenness disqualifies us. We are too shattered to belong. Others will reject us if they see our real wounds. But God's voice cuts through the noise with a different truth: You still belong. You are still Mine. And you were made for more than this.

Trauma often leads us to withdraw. I've seen it in my own life and in the lives of many others I've walked beside. Trauma doesn't just make us feel alone; it convinces us that we are alone, that no one could really understand what we're going through. What once felt like community now feels overwhelming. Trust feels risky. Small talk feels exhausting. We avoid eye contact, invitations, and even the people we love most. Sometimes, this isolation feels like a form of safety. But over time, it becomes a cage.

In the silence, we hear the ache of what was lost: our confidence, our sense of belonging, our identity. Yet in that same silence, God speaks.

He whispers that we were not created for isolation. Even in the Garden of Eden, before sin entered the world, God said, *"It is not good that the man should be alone"* (Genesis 2:18). That truth hasn't changed. Healing requires a relationship, not with everyone, but with someone.

**Isolation can become a barrier to growth. But it can also become a mirror.**

## Learning to Know Yourself Again

Disconnection from self often follows trauma just as certainly as disconnection from others. It isn't always obvious at first. It may begin with a sense of numbness, a loss of pleasure, or a dull ache in the soul that can't be named. Eventually, many trauma survivors look in the mirror and no longer recognize the person staring back at them.

This self-alienation happens because trauma reshapes the inner landscape. The person you were before feels inaccessible. You may wonder where that version of you went, or if they were ever real at all. You might catch yourself thinking, *"I used to be so joyful . . . I used to trust people . . . I used to laugh more."*

Reconnection, then, begins with grief. We must mourn the version of ourselves that trauma altered or took. That grief is sacred. God doesn't rush us through it. Instead, He sits with us in the ashes and gently says, *"You are still My beloved. You are not lost"*.

Reconnection doesn't just mean reaching out to others. It also means turning inward with honesty and compassion. Trauma can make us strangers to ourselves. As I've seen repeatedly in the healing process, trauma doesn't simply disrupt our daily lives; it fragments our internal narrative. It makes us question our instincts, doubt our resilience, and often feel like we have lost our core identity.

We forget what we enjoy. We lose track of who we were. Or we reject the past entirely, feeling as if the old version of us is unreachable or unworthy. But healing invites us to rediscover that we are not defined by what happened to us. The essential self, the one made in God's image, is still there, waiting to be known again.

Curiosity is where reconnection begins: "*What do I need today?*" "*What do I feel right now?*" "*What is one thing that brings me peace?*" It grows with self-compassion and grace for the slow process of becoming reacquainted with your own soul. Writing down what you feel or need may help. So does revisiting activities that once brought joy, music, art, nature, prayer, and community. You don't need to reclaim everything all at once. Even one small reconnection to yourself is a step in the right direction.

Healing also includes grieving the parts of you that feel distant or unreachable. The old version of you may never return exactly as they were, but something new, grounded, and beautiful can emerge from this place of rediscovery. It's not about becoming who you were. It's about becoming someone even more whole.

Even more, reconnecting with yourself means seeing your story through the eyes of grace. It's choosing to believe that your scars do not make you less than; they make you more real. Every line etched by pain is also a mark of survival, of endurance, of God's presence even when you didn't feel it. You are still becoming. And that becoming is sacred.

## Rebuilding Relationships

Human beings are wired for connection. From the very beginning, God designed us to live in relationship, with Him and with each other. But trauma distorts that design. It introduces fear where there was once trust, distance where there was once intimacy. And as much as we long for reconnection, it doesn't come easily.

Often, the most painful ruptures happen in the very relationships we assumed were safe. A betrayal by a friend. A failure by a caregiver. A rejection by a faith community. These breaks can leave lasting scars that make future connections feel risky, even dangerous. We might tell ourselves it's easier not to try again. But isolation is not God's plan for our healing. A relationship, even an imperfect, human, and vulnerable one, is part of the redemption story.

Rebuilding relationships doesn't begin with trust; it begins with honesty. By saying, *"I'm struggling,"* or *"This is hard for me."* Being willing to let someone see behind the mask, even if just a little. It also begins with healthy boundaries, where we learn to protect ourselves without shutting everyone out. Boundaries aren't walls; they're doors with hinges. And we get to decide when, how, and to whom we open them.

Reconnecting with others after trauma is delicate. Some relationships may not survive the rupture. Others will change. But a few, with time and effort, may deepen in ways you never expected.

Sometimes the people we love the most feel the most distant, not because we don't care, but because we're overwhelmed, guarded, or simply exhausted. That distance isn't always intentional, it's often a side effect of trying to protect ourselves. Even good intentions can become misunderstood, creating wedges between us and those we care about.

This kind of reconnection is built on honesty, boundaries, and mutual respect. It may mean admitting that you need help. It may mean saying, *"I'm not okay,"* or *"I don't know how to talk about this, but I want to try."* Real connection happens not through perfection, but through vulnerability.

Sometimes the bravest thing we can do is not rebuild a broken relationship, but allow a new one to begin, with healthier foundations and renewed trust. Rebuilding also includes knowing which relationships are no longer safe or sustainable. Reconnection always starts with truth and grace, both for ourselves and for those around us.

The truth about trust is that it can be lost in an instant. A single lie, a betrayal, a broken promise. It doesn't take much for trust to crumble. Rebuilding it, however, can take months, years, or a lifetime. Even when we forgive, something may still be lost. And even when we reconcile, the full return of intimacy isn't guaranteed. That's why many people, even when willing to forgive, remain cautious. Leery. Guarded. And that's okay. It's human.

But we must be honest with ourselves: trust, once broken, can't simply be restored with words. It must be rebuilt with actions, patience, humility, and consistency. And above all, grace. Whether trust is reformed, reimagined, or respectfully released, reconnection still has a role to play.

## Spiritual Reconnection

Reconnection with God can feel like the most complicated of all. We may have called out in our moment of trauma and heard nothing in return. That silence can feel like abandonment. Or worse, like rejection. It plants seeds of doubt not only in God's goodness but in our own worthiness. It's easy to wonder, if God really cared, why didn't He stop this? Or even, is this my punishment?

But those questions are not signs of faithlessness. They are the heart's desperate cry to make sense of a broken world. And God welcomes those cries. The Psalms are filled with them. Lament is not rebellion; it's relationship. It means we still believe God is there, and that He cares enough to listen.

**For many survivors, coming back to faith is not about certainty. It's about honesty.** It's about bringing the pain to God and saying, *"I don't understand, but I'm still reaching."* That act alone, of reaching, is sacred. Sometimes spiritual reconnection doesn't begin with prayer or church attendance. It begins with a breath. A sigh. A single verse that flickers in the darkness and refuses to go out. That spark is enough for God to work with.

There are moments when God feels distant. His goodness seems uncertain. Prayers feel like they fall flat. But these aren't signs of failure, they're the groanings of a soul reaching for hope. God isn't intimidated by the questions or shaken by the struggle. He meets you in the silence, in the ache, in the tension between doubt and desire. Like Jacob, who wrestled through the night and emerged with both a limp and a blessing, we too are shaped in the struggle. Changed, marked, and somehow held.

The spiritual journey after trauma seldom follows a straight path. There are days we feel the warmth of His nearness, and days when faith feels like a distant country. Sometimes, all we can offer is our confusion. But even that is enough. Even that becomes worship.

You do not have to feel holy to be held by God. He does not withdraw in your doubt. In fact, He draws closer. He welcomes the wounded, the uncertain, the weary, and He calls them His own.

If your faith has grown silent, begin again with one whispered Prayer *"God, I don't know where You are, but I want to find You."* He hears it. He treasures it. And He will meet you there.

## Reflection

Reconnection is not a single act; it's a journey. The process may be slow, uneven, and sometimes painful. But it is holy. You are not meant to live cut off and alone. You were created for communion, with others, with yourself, and with the God who still walks beside you. Every attempt at connection, no matter how small, is sacred ground.

Whether you're reaching for someone, reaching inward, or reaching heavenward, you are taking part in the redemptive act of restoration. Your willingness to try again, to hope again, is a declaration that trauma does not get the final word.

## Prayer

God, there are parts of me that feel so far away, from others, from You, even from myself. Trauma has isolated me, and I long to feel connected again. Help me take the next small step toward reconnection. Give me courage to reach out, grace to be patient, and faith to believe that restoration is possible. Help me to trust that even when I feel alone, I am not. Remind me that healing doesn't happen all at once, but in moments of grace, presence, and courage. Teach me how to reconnect with love, with gentleness, and with hope. Amen.

## Scripture

*"And the Lord God said, 'It is not good that the man should be alone.'"* Genesis 2:18

*"I am with you always, to the end of the age."* Matthew 28:20

*"He heals the brokenhearted and binds up their wounds."* Psalm 147:3

## Reflection Questions

1. How has trauma affected your connection with others?

_____

_____

_____

_____

_____

2. In what ways have you withdrawn from yourself emotionally or spiritually?

_____

_____

_____

_____

_____

3. Are there relationships worth rebuilding with grace and boundaries?

_____

_____

_____

_____

_____

4. What does spiritual reconnection look like for you right now?

_____

_____

_____

_____

_____

5. What small step could you take this week toward deeper connection?

_____

_____

_____

_____

_____

 Chapter 11:
# LEARNING TO RECEIVE LOVE AGAIN

Trauma teaches us how to survive, but hinders our ability to receive love. When wounds run deep, love can feel like a risk we can't afford to take. It can seem foreign, even suspicious. We become experts at withholding our hearts, retreating into emotional safety zones built to avoid further pain. And over time, the walls built for protection start to backfire, keeping out not just the hurt but also the very things our souls ache for: love, connection, and grace.

How do we learn to receive love again, not just from others, but from God and even from ourselves? It's not an easy process. The instinct to close off runs deep, especially when love has been distorted by betrayal, abandonment, or trauma. Yet, receiving love is not a sign of weakness; it is a courageous act of vulnerability and healing. It's how we remember who we truly are: beloved, seen, and chosen.

## Why Love Feels Dangerous

After trauma, love doesn't always feel like a gift. It can feel like a trap, a setup, or a threat. When we've been wounded by people we trusted, our brain learns to associate intimacy with danger. Acts of care feel unfamiliar. Compliments make us squirm. Kindness raises suspicion. Love asks us to open our hearts, but trauma has taught us that opening up gets us hurt.

That fear isn't irrational. It's protective. It's your nervous system trying to prevent future pain. But healing begins when we start to distinguish between past harm and present help. Just because someone in your past weaponized love doesn't mean that love itself is unsafe. Real love, the kind modeled by Christ, is not manipulative, conditional, or cruel. It's patient. It's kind. It keeps no record of wrongs. And yet, survivors often carry a hidden belief: I am not worthy of that kind of love.

## The Lie of Unworthiness

Trauma and shame often work together to convince us that we are not enough. They whisper that we are too impure, too weak, too unworthy of love. Once that belief takes root, receiving love becomes nearly impossible. Compliments are brushed aside. Acts of care are met with doubt. Even genuine kindness is filtered through a lens of suspicion. Love no longer feels like comfort. It feels like exposure.

Shame has a voice, and it's usually loudest in silence. It tells us to isolate. To push people away. To believe we must earn love through performance or perfection. But the truth of the gospel stands in direct opposition to that lie: *"But God shows His love for us in that while we were still sinners, Christ died for us"* (Romans 5:8).

His love transcends human logic; we don't earn it, nor do we deserve it. It's a gift, freely given, and only grace makes it possible to receive.

**We weren't loved because we got everything right. We were loved because God is good.**

## Why We Struggle to Receive

Some of us were never taught how to receive love well. We grew up earning approval through good behavior or performance. We learned that vulnerability was risky. Others of us had love withheld as a form of punishment. Or we experienced relationships where love came with strings attached. No wonder it's hard to trust love when it finally shows up freely.

Learning to receive love again requires unlearning these patterns. It's a rewiring of the heart and mind. That takes time. It takes gentleness. And it takes practice. For many survivors, it means confronting the fear that if we let love in, we will lose control. But true love doesn't seek to control. It seeks to heal.

## Letting God Love You

One of the hardest parts of trauma recovery is letting God love us, not just in theory, but in the raw, personal places. Many of us project the faces of our abusers or betrayers onto God. If a parent shamed us, we assume

God is shaming us too. If a spouse left us, we imagine God is on the verge of giving up as well.

But God's love is not like human love. *"As high as the heavens are above the earth, so great is his steadfast love toward those who fear him"* (Psalm 103:11). His love is not based on our behavior. It isn't scared off by our doubt or failure. He doesn't turn away from our scars. He draws near to them.

Receiving God's love is not about feeling worthy. It's about being willing. Willing to say, *"Even if I don't understand it, I want to believe it's true."* That mustard seed of faith is enough. God can work with that.

Receiving love from God also means surrendering the part of us that feels unlovable. We need to name the internal voice that says, *"You're too much,"* or *"we've gone too far."* God disagrees with that voice. In fact, He silences it. *"I have loved you with an everlasting love; therefore I have continued my faithfulness to you"* (Jeremiah 31:3). His love is not intimidated by our mess. He steps into it with grace.

## Receiving from Others

Healing always involves community. You weren't meant to walk this road alone. However, when we've been hurt by others, letting them back in can feel like a battlefield. That's okay. You don't have to do it all at once. Start small.

Receive the meal without apology. Hear the truth a friend offers without deflection. Stay in the embrace when the tears come, without shrinking back. These small moments of surrender are sacred. They teach your body that love is safe—and over time, they reshape the heart to recognize love not as danger, but as grace.

Receiving love doesn't mean becoming dependent. It means allowing others to share the burden. It means saying, *"I don't have to carry this alone."*

We can also learn to name what we need. That's not selfish, it's sacred clarity. *"I need space today." "I need someone to sit with me in silence." "I need a reminder that I'm not alone."* Safe people respond to those needs not with judgment but with grace.

## Receiving Love After Relational Betrayal

One of the most challenging wounds trauma inflicts is betrayal, when someone who was supposed to protect you becomes the one who hurts you. That kind of wound affects how we receive love. It teaches us to scan every relationship for hidden threats. It conditions us to expect rejection, manipulation, or abandonment.

After betrayal, love feels dangerous. Even when someone is trustworthy, we brace for disappointment. We flinch emotionally. We hold back. And sometimes we sabotage relationships before they can deepen.

But slowly, we can learn that not everyone is like the person who hurt us. Slowly, we can recognize that healthy love isn't about power or control; it's about mutual honor and safety. We rebuild trust with time, consistency, and truth. And we learn that even when we have been betrayed, we are still worthy of faithful love.

Forgiveness doesn't mean forgetting what happened. And reconciliation isn't always possible. But healing is. And healing often begins when we allow someone safe to love us in the places that have been hurt most.

## Receiving Love from Yourself

We talk a lot about loving others and receiving love from God, but what about love from ourselves? For many trauma survivors, self-love feels like a foreign concept, maybe even a selfish one. But true self-love isn't arrogance or self-centeredness. It's an agreement with God about your worth.

To receive love from yourself means learning to treat yourself with the same kindness, patience, and grace you would offer someone you care about. That might sound simple, but when we've been shaped by trauma, self-criticism often becomes a default setting. Mistakes replay in your mind on a loop. The pressure to heal quickly often leads to self-blame. Control becomes the goal, and impossible standards feel like the only way to stay safe.

But Jesus didn't die for a future, perfect version of you. He died for you, as you are. And if God calls you beloved, who are you to argue?

- Receiving love from yourself may look like:

- Choosing rest without guilt.

- Speaking to yourself with gentleness, not judgment.

- Setting boundaries that honor your capacity.

- Allowing space for your emotions without shame.

- Refusing to measure your healing by someone else's timeline.

Every time you choose grace over harshness, you're practicing self-love. And the more you learn to love yourself in a healthy way, the more freely you'll be able to receive love from others.

## Healing Through the Body

Love isn't just a mental or emotional experience; it's physical, too. Trauma is stored in the body, and often, so is our resistance to love. Our bodies learn to react to perceived threats with tension, withdrawal, dissociation, and flinching, even after the threat has passed.

*Part of learning to receive love again is inviting your body into the healing process. That might mean:

*Practicing grounding techniques to help you stay present during moments of care.

*Letting yourself be hugged, even if it feels awkward at first.

*Noticing when your shoulders tense or your breathing shortens in response to affection and choosing to soften.

*Engaging in safe touch, movement, or breathwork to reconnect with safety.

*Your body is not your enemy. It has fought to protect you. Now, you get to teach it that love can be safe again.

## When Love Feels Unearned

One of the most humbling parts of recovery is realizing you can't earn the kind of love your soul most needs. Grace, by nature, is unearned. It's not a transaction. It's a gift. And for many, receiving a gift like that feels unsettling. There's a part of us that wants to earn love so we can feel we deserve it.

But God's love was never based on your performance. It has always been based on His character.

You're not loved because we've arrived. You're loved right here—in the mess, in the ache, in the trembling. Healing isn't a prerequisite. All that's asked is a heart open enough to receive. Earned love breeds fear, but love given freely, by grace, becomes a refuge no storm can undo.

## The Discipline of Receptivity

**Receiving love is more than a feeling; it's a spiritual discipline.**

Just like prayer, worship, or Scripture meditation, it's something we grow into through repeated, intentional practice. For those of us who are used to giving, fixing, or hiding, learning to receive can feel deeply unnatural. But like any discipline, it becomes more familiar over time.

Receptivity is a posture of humility. It's saying, *"I can't do this alone. I need help. I need grace. I need love, I didn't earn."* That can be hard to admit, especially if independence has been your survival strategy. But healing doesn't happen in isolation. It happens when we let love in, when we open the gates, even if just a crack, and allow someone else's light to reach the parts of us still hidden in shadow.

This kind of receptivity doesn't mean being passive or powerless. It means being open, open to care, to truth, to beauty, to healing. It means releasing the armor we've outgrown and trusting that God is not waiting to punish our weakness, but to meet us in it with compassion.

Start small. When someone tells you that you matter, resist the urge to brush it off; just say thank you. When God speaks the quiet truth, *"You are Mine,"* lean in instead of turning away. And when a flicker of self-compassion rises in your own heart, don't silence it. Let it settle. Let it stay.

Receptivity is holy. It's how we begin to believe what's been true all along: l we were never meant to earn love; we were meant to abide in it.

## Reflection

Receiving love is not passive; it's powerful. It's an act of resistance against shame, fear, and isolation. To receive love again is to say, *"I am still worthy of belonging. I am still God's child. I still carry sacred value."*

You may be learning slowly. You may take steps forward and then pull back. That's okay. This is not a race. Even the smallest act of receiving, one hug, one kind word, one whispered prayer, is a victory. Let the walls come down. Not all at once, but brick by brick. Let grace in.

## Prayer

Father, You see the places in me that are still closed off. You know the hurt that taught me to be guarded. And yet, You call me to receive, not just Your love, but the love of others. Help me trust again. Help me believe that I am not too broken to be cared for. That I don't have to earn love, I only have to receive it. Teach me to open my hands, my heart, and my life. Surround me with safe people. Heal the memories that taught me love was dangerous. Let Your perfect love cast out my fear. Amen.

## Scripture

"*There is no fear in love, but perfect love casts out fear.*" 1 John 4:18

"*We love because he first loved us.*" 1 John 4:19

"*But God shows his love for us in that while we were still sinners, Christ died for us.*" Romans 5:8

"*I have loved you with an everlasting love; therefore, I have continued my faithfulness to you.*" Jeremiah 31:3

## Reflection Questions

1.  What makes it difficult for you to receive love?

 

 

 

 

2.  In what ways has trauma distorted your view of love?

 

 

 

 

3.  How have you seen God's love break through your defenses?

 

 

 

4. Who in your life is safe to practice receiving love from?

_____

_____

_____

_____

_____

5. What would it look like to open your heart a little more this week?

_____

_____

_____

_____

_____

Chapter 12:
# REBUILDING IDENTITY AFTER TRAUMA

Trauma doesn't just wound the body or emotions; it fractures the sense of self. After trauma, we often lose sight of who we are. We become the sum of what happened to us. The person in the mirror looks familiar but feels foreign. We may wonder, *"Am I still me? Or am I just what's left?"*

Reclaiming identity after trauma isn't a single moment of clarity. It's a slow, sacred process of remembering who we truly are—not the version shaped by fear or loss, but the one grounded in truth. Healing unfolds the same way harm was done: moment by moment, thought by thought, with grace guiding the way.

## The Shattered Mirror

For some of us, the fracture of identity after trauma is subtle. Rather than a dramatic collapse, it unfolds as a slow erosion. Needs we once recognized become harder to name. The ability to speak up fades. Moments that used to stir passion or joy now feel muted. It's as if someone gradually dimmed the light switch on our inner lives, and we didn't notice until everything turned gray.

Others among us feel the shatter all at once, like waking up in a body we no longer trust, with emotions we can't name, in a life that no longer fits. Panic attacks may hit without warning. Mirrors and photos can feel unbearable because they reflect someone we don't recognize. And in the quiet moments, we ask ourselves, *"Is this who I am now?"*

No matter how the fracture showed up, the restoration process begins the same way: with truth, kindness, and patience. Begin by learning to recognize what's yours and what was forced upon you, with the belief that healing isn't about becoming who you were, it's about becoming who you really are.

Trauma distorts the way we see ourselves. You may feel broken, ashamed, or unrecognizable. You might define yourself by your failures, your wounds, or the labels others put on you. These distortions become like a shattered mirror: every piece reflects a part of the story, but none shows the whole truth.

Shame insists your value was erased by what you went through. But shame lies. Our identity is not rooted in the pain you carried, the harm done to you, or the ways you had to adapt just to make it through. None of that defines you. It never did.

Healing invites you to pick up each broken piece and ask, *"What is true? What needs to be released?"* Then slowly, with grace, begin to rebuild. Sometimes trauma builds a false self, one designed to perform, protect, or disappear. We become caretakers, perfectionists, or wallflowers. These parts helped us survive. But survival is not the same as living. To truly heal, we must separate who we are from who we had to be.

You may find yourself saying, *"I don't even know who I am anymore."* That's not failure. That's honesty. And it's a good place to start. Discovering who you are now isn't about recreating the past. It's about meeting yourself again, in light of the truth and love that's been present all along.

## Who Were You Before the Wound?

In one story shared by a survivor, she described herself as a *"ghost walking through her own life"* after years of abuse. She didn't know what she liked anymore. Her decisions were driven by fear or a desire for appeasement. And yet, in therapy, something unexpected happened. Her therapist asked her to make a playlist, not of her trauma, but of who she was before.

What began as a strange exercise became a turning point. The music she had forgotten made her cry, then smile. It reminded her of joy, of dancing in the kitchen, of the girl who used to believe she was loved. That girl wasn't gone, just buried. Remembering her was an act of resurrection.

Sometimes restoration begins quietly, with a journal entry, a familiar meal, a long-forgotten photograph, or a whispered prayer in the dark. These aren't trivial moments. They are sacred. They gently lead you back to yourself, reminding you that while trauma may have shaped parts of your story, it never had the authority to name you.

Who you were before still matters, but even more, who you are becoming now matters deeply. God doesn't simply return you to your former self; He leads you toward who you were always meant to be. Healing sometimes begins with remembering: What once brought you joy? What stirred your passion? What did you believe about God, the world, and your place in it? We may not be able to return to that version of ourselves, but you can honor them. We can grieve what was lost, carry forward what was good, and let God restore what shame tried to erase.

Remembering isn't about nostalgia. To remember is an act of reconnection. It gathers the fragments of your story that were buried beneath fear, silence, or shame. Moments of joy. Glimpses of innocence. Traces of hope that still live within you. Gently ask God to uncover those memories, not just to mourn them, but to reclaim the most genuine parts of yourself. We never lost them; we only hid them.

*"Therefore, if anyone is in Christ, he is a new creation. The old has passed away; behold, the new has come"* (2 Corinthians 5:17).

## Naming the Lies

Part of trauma's cruelty is that it teaches us not only to expect harm, but to believe we deserve it. It wires us to interpret kindness as manipulation and acceptance as a trap. Over time, these interpretations harden into identity. What began as a defense becomes a belief system. What was once a coping mechanism becomes a lens we can't see beyond.

We have to face the internal dialogue that has run unchecked for years. The one that says, *"No one really wants you."* Or, *"You'll be rejected if they see the real you."* These voices aren't intuition. They're echoes of the past, and they do not speak for your future.

**Healing doesn't start with affirmation; it starts with confrontation.**

Healing requires naming the lies that trauma taught you. Maybe you believe:

- "I'm too damaged."

- *"I'm weak."*

- "I'm unlovable."

- *"I'll never be safe."*

These aren't truths. They're wounds pretending to be facts.

*The truth is*:

- *You are more than what hurts you.*

- *You survived. That is a strength.*

- *You are deeply loved, even when you don't feel it.*

## Safety Can Be Rebuilt

As you begin to name the lies trauma taught you, replace them boldly and intentionally with truth. Anchor yourself in Scripture. Speak with your own voice. Borrow the voices of those who love you and see you clearly. Say those truths out loud until they begin to sink in. Write them down. Return to them often. Let them play in the background of your days like a quiet anthem of healing. *"The truth will set you free"* isn't just

**Declaring the truth takes it back.**

about salvation—it's about recovery. Naming the lie takes away its power. Healing begins not in denial, but in deliverance—when you stop agreeing with shame and start aligning with the voice of God.

## Living into the Truth

Living out your true identity isn't a one-time decision; it's a daily return. It's waking up each morning and asking, *"What's true about me today?" before* the voices of shame or fear answer first. You may not always feel like someone who is beloved, chosen, and free, but you can still live like it's true.

We reclaim identity by choosing small acts of agreement with truth. That might mean saying yes to rest instead of running on exhaustion to prove our worth. It could mean stepping away from relationships that ask us to shrink, or speaking truth to ourselves even when it feels unfamiliar. Sometimes it looks like letting others care for us, praying when isolation feels safer, or returning to Scripture when our thoughts begin to spiral. These choices, though small, are sacred. They slowly rebuild what trauma tried to take.

These aren't grand gestures; they're daily habits of healing. Each one reinforces the truth of who you are. Each one tells your brain, your body, and your spirit: I don't belong to trauma anymore. I belong to God.

## Identity in Christ

Healing our identity means more than stopping the lies; it means learning to live inside the truth. This is not about conjuring up self-esteem; it's about receiving God's revelation. We are who He says we are. But that can feel unfamiliar at first. When trauma has been our teacher, safety feels like risk. Rest feels like exposure. Even love feels too vulnerable. So instead of rushing to "feel" new, we practice believing what's already true, little by little.

Some days, that belief will come easily. Other days, it will feel like lifting spiritual weights. Don't mistake struggle for failure. Every time we agree with God over our shame, even in a whisper, we reclaim sacred ground. There's a reason trauma attacks our identity; it knows that if it can confuse who we are, it can shake everything else. But God doesn't leave our identity up to our pain, our past, or our performance. He anchors it in Himself.

God formed us in His image, not trauma's shadow. Long before the pain, there was a deeper truth. We were created to reflect His goodness, to carry His love, to live in freedom. And even now, that truth remains. Nothing we've been through disqualifies us. Nothing lost makes us less His. We are still seen, still chosen, still held.

One of the most powerful steps in recovery is learning to anchor our identity not in what happened to us, but in who we are in Christ. In Him, we are not defined by our wounds. We are chosen, redeemed, forgiven, and made whole. This isn't wishful thinking. It's the truth spoken by the One who cannot lie. Trauma may have altered the shape of our story, but it no longer holds the pen. God does. And He calls us beloved.

Even when we don't feel worthy, we can still agree with God: *I am who You say I am.* Let His voice interrupt the noise in our mind. Let grace be the mirror we look into—not the broken one, but the one that reflects what's true. We are not our symptoms. Not our setbacks. Not the labels others placed on us. We belong to God. That is our most authentic identity. *"You are precious in my eyes, and honored, and I love you"* (Isaiah 43:4).

When we lose our sense of self, we often lose our direction. That's why rebuilding identity isn't just about self-worth, it's about finding our way again. If trauma stripped away our sense of value, God is gently handing it back. Not because we earned it, but because it was never meant to be taken in the first place.

We were always meant to live a life of love. When identity is restored, confidence begins to return, not arrogance, but assurance. A quiet strength rooted in knowing who you are and Whose you are. Let your healing be shaped, not by pressure to be the person you were, but by the invitation to become someone deeper, truer, and more whole than we've ever been. The world will try to rename you based on your scars. But God calls you by your redeemed name. The more you say yes to the truth, the more the lies lose their power. The more you walk in who you are, the more you heal.

It isn't about rewriting your past, it's about reclaiming your future. You don't have to keep living under false identities. Let God do the slow, holy work of revealing the real you. You are not a problem to fix; you are a person being restored. Your identity is not what happened to you. It is who you are becoming through grace.

Take time to remember who you truly are. Not the version shaped by trauma. Not the identity fear tries to assign. Beneath the wounds and the worry is a person created with purpose, dignity, and strength. That is the identity worth returning to. But who God declares you to be. Ask Him to reintroduce you to yourself.

## Practicing the Shift

The journey from false identity to true self is not a straight line. It's a winding road filled with tension. You might move forward and then suddenly feel like you're back where you started. That doesn't mean you're failing. It means you're healing.

One way to solidify identity is through intentional practices. These don't have to be rigid or performative. They simply create space for the truth to settle deeper.

Here are a few:

Mirror Truth Practice: Each morning, look in the mirror and speak one truth about your identity aloud. For example, *"I am chosen. I am not what happened to me."*

Name the Lie and Replace It: When you catch yourself thinking, *"I'll always be broken,"* pause and say, *"That's not true. I am being restored."*

Keep a Truth Journal: Write down the moments you feel most aligned with your true self after a meaningful conversation, during worship, or when setting a boundary. These are glimpses of who you are. These simple acts reinforce your identity from the inside out. Over time, they help you live more fully into who you already are.

## Reflection

Rebuilding your identity after trauma isn't about becoming who you were, it's about discovering who you truly are. Trauma may have shaken your sense of self, but it never erased your worth. Beneath the pain and survival patterns, God still sees you clearly: loved, chosen, His.

This journey isn't quick or easy. But every time you say yes to truth over lies, you reclaim a piece of yourself. Each small act of courage, setting a boundary, receiving kindness, speaking Scripture aloud, echoes your true identity. You are not what happened to you. You are not the roles you played to stay safe. You are who God says you are. Let His voice be louder than the past. Let grace become your mirror. And let Him gently lead you back to yourself.

## Prayer

God, help me see myself through Your eyes. I've carried false names for too long: Broken. Unworthy. Too much. Not enough. But You call me by a different name: Beloved. Teach me to believe it. Show me who I truly am. Help me release the shame and wear the identity we've given me, whole, chosen, and made new. Let me trust that I am not my worst day. I am not my trauma. I am not who they said I was. I am Yours. Reveal the truth beneath the rubble. Speak over me the name we've always known. Amen.

## Scripture

*"You are no longer a slave, but a son, and if a son, then an heir through God."* Galatians 4:7

*"The Spirit himself bears witness with our spirit that we are children of God."* Romans 8:16

*"I have called you by name, you are mine."* Isaiah 43:1

*"For we are his workmanship, created in Christ Jesus for good works . . . "* Ephesians 2:10

*"You are precious in my eyes, and honored, and I love you."* Isaiah 43:4

## Reflection Questions

1. How has trauma distorted the way you see yourself?

2. What parts of your identity do you want God to restore?

_____

_____

_____

_____

_____

3. How does God's view of you challenge your view of yourself?

_____

_____

_____

_____

_____

4. Where do you still struggle to believe you are more than what happened to you?

_____

_____

_____

_____

_____

5. What step can you take this week to reflect the truth of who you really are?

_____

_____

_____

_____

_____

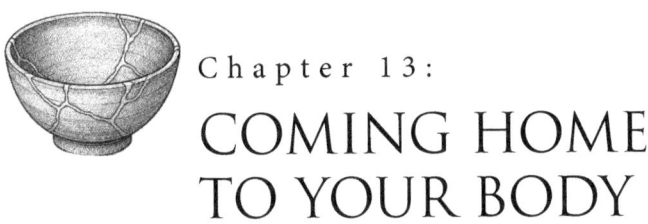

Chapter 13:

# COMING HOME TO YOUR BODY

For many trauma survivors, the body doesn't feel like home; it feels like a threat. It carries memories you didn't ask for. Sensations you can't explain. And reactions that don't make sense, even to you. The very place meant to hold safety instead feels like the site of harm.

Healing often involves the slow, sacred work of learning to inhabit our bodies again. Not just surviving in them, but feeling safe within them. It means no longer running from ourselves, but returning to the body—not as an enemy to fight, but as a companion in the healing process.

## When the Body Remembers What the Mind Forgets

**There are moments when your body tells the truth long before your mind catches up.** A smell that brings on a wave of panic. A place that makes your skin crawl. A raised voice that tightens your muscles even if the words aren't directed at you. These aren't overreactions. They're unresolved signals.

The nervous system, beautifully designed by God, protects us in crisis by compartmentalizing. We don't always remember everything. Numbness may settle in as a form of mercy. Often, our bodies carry what our minds cannot yet understand. Your nervous system isn't the enemy. It's working hard to protect you, doing exactly what it was designed to do. It remembers what happened, even when the conscious mind cannot fully explain it. Patterns of tension, hypervigilance, or withdrawal are its way of guarding against future harm. But what once offered safety may now be the very thing keeping us stuck, trapped in fear rather than moving toward healing.

This is the complexity of trauma: your body responds as if the threat is still happening, even when you're safe. That gap between past and present can be exhausting. And confusing. And discouraging. But it's also the gap where healing can take place.

Trauma is not just something that happens to us; it imprints on us. Long after the event has passed, the body remembers. A tightness in your chest may rise for no apparent reason. Sudden sounds might make you flinch. Even a gentle touch can cause you to go numb. The impact lingers, woven into the nervous system, echoing long after the danger is gone.

These are not signs of weakness. They're signs of a nervous system doing its best to protect you. Your body has learned survival patterns, even if they no longer serve you.

We often think of healing as a mental or emotional task. But the body must heal, too. It needs to know that the danger is over. And that starts with learning to listen.

## The Disconnection

Disconnection doesn't always look dramatic. It can manifest in subtle ways, such as ignoring hunger cues or pushing past the need for rest. You might find yourself overworking because stillness feels unbearable, or mindlessly scrolling through your phone instead of noticing the tightness in your chest. Trauma teaches us to disconnect not only from pain, but from the body itself.

And when we live from that place of disconnection, it affects everything. It's harder to know what we need. Harder to advocate for ourselves. Harder to believe we're worth caring for. However, the good news is that if trauma has taught us to disconnect, healing can teach us to reconnect.

One of trauma's first casualties is the connection to the body. You may have learned to disassociate, to leave your body when it felt too unsafe to stay. This was not a failure. It was a survival response. But over time, this disconnection can make it hard to know what you feel, what you need, or even where you hurt. Reconnection doesn't happen overnight. But it is possible. Through small, intentional practices, you can begin to feel again. To notice again. To trust again.

## Practices That Help You Return

Returning to the body is not a one-time decision. It is a lifelong rhythm. The practices may seem simple at first, but over time, they become sacred. These embodied rituals are not about performance. They are invitations: permission to rest, permission to feel, permission to be.

Reconnection to the body doesn't come from intellectual insight alone, it requires lived experience. The body needs evidence that it is no longer under threat. It needs new memories, new cues of safety, and new rituals of care. What you practice consistently, your nervous system begins to believe.

Reconnection is not about doing everything perfectly; it's about building new rhythms of safety. Each time you pause to notice your breath, you are choosing presence. Each time you stretch instead of shutting down, you are making space for healing.

## What God Says about the Body

Your body has always been part of God's story. From the dust of Eden to the wounds of Christ, Scripture affirms that flesh is not an afterthought; it is beloved. God crafted the body with intention and dignity. He called it good.

When trauma causes you to feel alien in your own skin, God doesn't stand at a distance demanding you fix yourself. He draws near. He meets you not in the abstract, but in your embodiment. In the breath you take when you calm down. In the stillness after we've let ourselves cry, in the trembling that begins to slow as you feel safe.

Jesus, fully God and fully human, had a human body. He embraced hunger, touch, fatigue, and pain. And through His body, He brought healing to others. This is not accidental, but a model. It's a declaration that our bodies are not obstacles to be managed, but sacred ground where God meets us.

God designed our bodies not as distractions from spiritual life, but as participants in it. The body is where we experience joy, grief, rest, love, and presence. When Scripture calls the body a temple, it isn't offering a metaphor for perfection; it's offering a truth about holiness.

Holiness doesn't mean flawlessness. It means set apart. Sacred. That includes your body, even with its scars, its stories, its survival. Scripture doesn't treat the body as disposable. It calls it a temple. A vessel. A dwelling place for the Spirit of God. Your body matters, not just as a physical shell, but as a part of your healing. God doesn't reject your body because of what it's been through. He draws near. Jesus touched lepers, dined with the shamed, and healed the wounded.

**Jesus' ministry was physical. Embodied. Present. He still meets us in the flesh and bone. In our breath. In our tension. In our healing.**

## You Don't Have to Rush

There is no finish line in this kind of healing. There's only the next gentle step. Some days, that step might look like getting out of bed. Other days, it might be choosing not to criticize your reflection. Still other days, it may be allowing someone to hug you without flinching. Each of these is sacred. Each one is a kind of homecoming.

Remember, your body is not behind. It's not failing. It's responding with the wisdom it gathered during your toughest moments. You don't need to shame that wisdom; you need to help it evolve. As you begin to inhabit your body with more presence, offer yourself compassion. When old responses rise up, pause and ask, *"What is my body trying to tell me?"*

You may not always understand the answer, but the act of listening is an essential part of the healing process. The goal isn't to force comfort, but to nurture safety. Reclaiming safety in your body is not a race. Some days you may feel progress. Other days, you may feel set back. That's okay. Healing is non-linear. What matters is the direction, not the speed. Celebrate small wins when you realize your breath. The time you stayed present during a hard conversation. The day you chose rest over punishment. These are sacred moments. Mark them. Coming home to your body isn't about forcing comfort. It's about choosing presence.

## Creating a Safe Inner Environment

Our bodies often carry the echoes of every harsh word turned inward. We don't just inherit shame from others; we rehearse it within. But healing can't flourish in an environment of self-contempt. We must learn to offer the same compassion to ourselves that we would give to a hurting friend.

Creating a safe inner environment means learning to respond to pain with presence rather than punishment. Instead of spiraling when your heart races, pause and breathe. When your body aches, offer care instead of neglect. As fear rises, respond with compassion rather than criticism. These small, consistent choices don't erase the trauma, but they begin to rewire how you respond to it. Over time, your body starts to associate presence with kindness—and eventually, with peace.

As your relationship with your body changes, so will the way you speak to yourself. One of the most overlooked aspects of healing is self-talk. The words you say inwardly matter. Would you talk to a child the way you speak to yourself? Would you dismiss their fear or belittle their pain?

This is not just about being kind, it's about being safe. Your inner environment shapes your ability to stay present. If your body is no longer a battlefield, then your thoughts can become a refuge, not another place of war. Try beginning your day with one small, kind statement. It might feel foreign. That's okay. Most healing does at first. Keep showing up with gentleness, and over time, the language of grace will take root.

The body doesn't only remember pain, it also remembers joy. That memory may feel out of reach right now, but it's still there. Joy lives in the laugh you didn't hold back. In the warmth of sunlight on your face. Dancing barefoot in the kitchen. These aren't silly moments, they're sacred ones. Signs that your body isn't just surviving; it's beginning to live again. As you heal, look for moments of embodied joy and let them count. Let them sink in. Let your nervous system experience what safety and celebration feel like again. These are not distractions from healing. They *are* healing.

## The Body and Boundaries

Part of coming home to our body is learning to protect it, not out of fear, but from a place of value. Boundaries are not walls to keep everyone out. They are gates that let safety in. They are the physical and emotional spaces you define so that your body can breathe, your heart can rest, and your spirit can heal.

Many survivors never learned they had a right to boundaries. Maybe our *"no"* was ignored. Maybe we were punished for having needs, or maybe love came with conditions. Over time, your body learned to tolerate discomfort rather than risk conflict. But healing means learning a new pattern.

You are allowed to say no without explanation. We are allowed to leave spaces that feel unsafe, and we are allowed to speak up when something hurts. These aren't selfish acts; they are sacred ones. And each time we practice a boundary, our body receives a message: You matter. You are safe with me. Boundaries are how we create safety from the inside out. These practices aren't just for others. They're for you. They offer relief to a nervous system that has been on guard for too long. In their quiet consistency, they begin to rebuild the safety that trust needs in order to take root again.

## Embodied Belonging

Belonging is not just an emotional need, it's a physical one. The nervous system seeks cues of connection, safety, and acceptance. When you are in a place where you are seen, welcomed, and not judged, your body relaxes. Your breath deepens. Your guard lowers.

That's why spiritual belonging must include embodied safety. It's not enough to say you belong to God. Your body has to learn it. That might happen in worship, in communion, in silence, or in community. But wherever it happens, it must involve the whole person, when you begin to feel that belonging in your bones, not just your beliefs, you will move through the world differently. You'll carry yourself not in defense, but in dignity.

Healing in the body isn't meant to happen in isolation. We need safe people, those who honor our "no" and celebrate our "*yes*". People who won't rush our healing or shame our pace. Embodied healing in community means being seen not just for what we've survived, but for who we are becoming.

It might mean sitting silently beside a friend who doesn't try to fix you. Or walking alongside someone whose trauma doesn't mirror yours, but whose compassion makes space for it anyway. When we practice presence with each other, we model the kind of safety our bodies crave.

The church, at its best, is a place where bodies are honored and not judged, not ignored. Not treated as distractions, but held as holy. When we show up with our bodies, tired, trembling, healing, hoping, we reflect the Incarnation. We bear witness to a God who did not stay distant but entered into flesh.

This is the invitation: to be present, not just to yourself, but to others. To let your body relearn trust in the safety of real connection.

## The Body as Witness

Your body is not just a container of pain, it's a witness to your survival. Every heartbeat, every breath, every scar, every stretch mark, and line on your face is evidence: you lived. You endured. You are still here. That deserves reverence. That deserves care.

Too often, we treat the body like something to fix or punish. We drive it past its limits. Ignore its cries for nourishment. Shame it for needing rest. But what if the body isn't broken? What if it's doing exactly what it was designed to do, alerting you, grounding you, protecting you?

To honor the body is to listen to its language. Fatigue might mean you need rest, not more caffeine. Anxiety might be a signal to slow down, not push harder. Hunger might be about more than food, it might be about presence, connection, pleasure, peace. The more you attend to these cues, the more you learn your body's wisdom. It stops being a problem to solve and starts becoming a partner in the healing process.

## Reflection

Coming home to your body isn't just a healing task; it's a spiritual practice. Each breath taken without fear, each moment of grounded presence, each boundary set in kindness—these are ways of reclaiming sacred ground. Your body has been a battlefield, but it can become a sanctuary. Let it be a place where you meet God, not beyond the pain, but right in the middle of it.

## Prayer

God, I confess that my body feels like a stranger to me. I've lived disconnected, afraid, and ashamed of what it holds. But You made this body. You call it good. You call it Yours. Teach me to return to it. To listen without judgment. To care for it with gentleness. To believe that even here, especially here, You dwell. Restore my relationship with the body You gave me. Let it become not a place of panic, but of peace. Amen.

## Reflection Questions

1.  What messages have you received about your body from trauma?

_____

_____

_____

_____

2.  When do you feel most disconnected from your body?

_____

_____

_____

_____

3. What small practice could help you begin to feel safer in your body today?

_____

_____

_____

_____

_____

4. How does God's view of your body differ from your own?

_____

_____

_____

_____

5. What would it look like to treat your body as a place of healing, not harm?

_____

_____

_____

_____

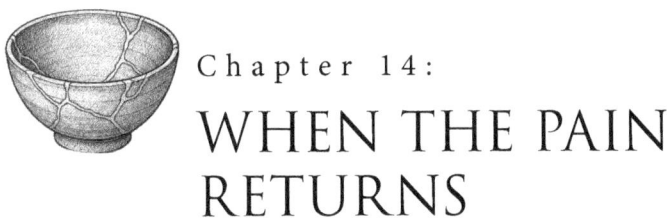

Chapter 14:

# WHEN THE PAIN RETURNS

There's a moment in every healing journey that feels like betrayal. We prayed. We cried. We did the hard work in therapy sessions, Scripture reading, and support groups. We kept showing up. Some of us even stood before others and shared our stories. There were breakthrough moments when hope lit up the darkness, when it felt like we had finally made it to the other side of the wound.

Then, without warning, the ache returns. A phrase catches us off guard. A familiar smell. A room that feels too much like before. Suddenly, we are back there. Our hearts race, shoulders tense, breath grows shallow, and pain spreads across our chest like a fire we thought had long since gone out.

For many trauma survivors, the return of pain feels like failure. It can seem as if all the progress has unraveled in an instant, as though the scar we've tried to wear with honor has been torn open again. But what if the re-emergence of pain isn't a setback? What if it's a deeper layer of healing rising to the surface—an invitation to tend to what was never fully seen or soothed the first time?

## Healing Is Not a Straight Line

The image many people carry of recovery is that it moves upward, like climbing a staircase, each step a little higher than the one before. But trauma doesn't follow neat patterns. The path isn't straight. It spirals, loops back on itself, dips without warning, then climbs again. Sometimes it surprises us, not just with pain, but with progress we didn't expect. The work of healing is more like walking a labyrinth than scaling a mountain. You circle around familiar places, not because you're lost, but because you're going deeper.

When the pain returns, it's not proof we've failed. It may be a sign that your soul finally feels safe enough to surface what was too painful to process before. The nervous system, beautifully designed by God, protects us in crisis by compartmentalizing. We don't always remember everything. Numbness may settle in as a form of mercy. Often, our bodies carry what our minds cannot yet understand. But as healing unfolds, layer by layer, memories may return. Emotions rise. The pain that revisits you may actually be an invitation to receive grace in the places you once sealed off.

Jesus Himself understood this kind of return. After His resurrection, He bore His scars, not as open wounds, but as markers of His passage through suffering. He invited Thomas to touch them. *"Put your finger here, and see my hands*" (John 20:27). The pain had passed, but the scars remained, testifying to both suffering and survival. In your own journey, when the pain returns, you too are being invited to touch the wound with new eyes, not as a prisoner of the past, but as someone who is learning to live, love, and lead from a place of deeper wholeness.

Alyssa had come a long way. She'd left the abusive relationship and worked through childhood trauma with a counselor. Worship leading had become part of her life again. Her smile was returning. For the first time in a long while, she felt alive. But one afternoon, while walking through a parking garage, the sharp slam of a car door echoed behind her, and her breath caught. Her body went stiff. Fear surged. Tears welled up. Her heart pounded, and she had no idea why.

Later, she realized: the sound, the echo, the moment, it all matched the night she'd first tried to run. "*I thought I was past this,*" she whispered in therapy the next day. "*I thought I'd already healed.*" Her counselor replied, "*You have. This isn't failure. It's your body telling you that there's still more to release, and you're strong enough now to do it.*" That moment marked a turning point in Alyssa's recovery. She began practicing trauma-informed grounding techniques. She memorized Psalm 34:18: "*The Lord is near to the brokenhearted and saves the crushed in spirit.*" And slowly, she learned that when pain returns, it's not her undoing, it's her deepening.

## Understanding Triggers and Flashbacks

In the chapter entitled "The Grief Trauma Leaves Behind," we learned about triggers, but more needs to be said on this topic. Triggers can be subtle or overwhelming. A song, a scent, a season, or even a person's tone of voice can carry you back to trauma's doorstep. Flashbacks, whether emotional or physical, are not imaginary. They are your body's way of warning you that it recognizes danger, even if that danger is no longer present.

It can be frustrating. You might feel crazy or weak. But you're not. This is your nervous system doing its best to protect you. The problem is, trauma scrambles the alarm system. Your brain's amygdala may react to the present moment as if it were the original threat. The key is not to shame yourself, but gently to remind your body and spirit: *"This is not then. I am safe now."*

When the pain returns, try not to meet it with judgment. Instead, approach it with curiosity and kindness. Ask yourself, *What is my body trying to tell me? What emotion is surfacing that needs attention? What part of my story still needs God's healing touch?* Healing often requires us to circle back, not to remain in the pain, but to gently reclaim what was lost, one piece at a time, with compassion and care.

## Practices for Navigating the Return

Here are some grounding tools and spiritual practices to hold you steady when the pain resurfaces:

- Breath Prayer – Inhale a phrase of Scripture or grace (e.g., *"Peace of Christ . . ."*), exhale a release". . . *wash over me"*.

- Body Awareness – Name where you feel the pain. Is it in your chest? Shoulders? Hands? Gently place a hand there and breathe.

- Scripture Anchoring – Choose a verse you can return to when you feel disoriented. Let it be a lifeline. *"When I am afraid, I put my trust in you"* (Psalm 56:3).

- Soothing Rituals – Light a candle. Play a favorite worship song. Wrap yourself in a blanket. These physical gestures tell your body, *"We are safe now."*

- Journaling What Comes Up – Instead of pushing away the resurgence of pain, write it out. Give language to the flashback or the feeling. *"I pour out my complaint before him; I tell my trouble before him"* (Psalm 142:2).

- Safe Person Contact – Reach out to someone who "gets it." A trauma-informed friend, a spiritual companion, or a counselor can remind you that you're not alone. *"Bear one another's burdens, and so fulfill the law of Christ"* (Galatians 6:2).

## Scars Revisited

There is a reason the resurrected Christ still bore scars. He could have come back flawless. Instead, He returned in a body marked by love and pain. His scars were not weaknesses. They were witnesses.

As the apostle Paul writes, "We are afflicted in every way, but not crushed; perplexed, but not driven to despair . . . struck down, but not destroyed" (2 Corinthians 4:8-9). There will be days when the ache comes roaring back. But the One who raised Christ from the dead lives in you. That power does not disappear just because pain reappears.

The scar is not shameful. It is testimony. Let it speak.

**The returning pain may be a scar that's learning how to breathe again, not because it's breaking open, but because it's releasing the last of what it was holding.**

## The Invitation Hidden in the Ache

Pain that returns is not always a problem to be solved; it may be a messenger to be listened to. It might be revealing an area of our life that needs rest. Or a relationship that needs boundaries. Or an old lie we didn't realize still lived under the surface.

God's healing work often goes deeper than we expect. It's not just about making the pain go away. It's about transformation. As Paul writes to the Romans, *"Do not be conformed to this world, but be transformed by the renewal of your mind"* (Romans 12:2). That kind of renewal isn't just cognitive. It's emotional. Spiritual. Even physical. And it doesn't happen all at once.

So when the pain returns, receive it as an invitation, not to return to despair, but to return to grace. God isn't finished with you yet. Not when the pain first came. Not when you first found healing. And not now. He is faithful in the first breakthrough, and He is faithful in every return.

Daniel was a former military chaplain, a man who had seen too much and felt too deeply. Years after retiring, he'd found peace again, or so he thought. He led a quiet life now: gardening, teaching Sunday School, and occasionally officiating weddings. But one Sunday morning, a visiting veteran sat in the front pew, head bowed. During the closing hymn, Daniel saw the man tremble, just slightly, and something in him cracked wide open. He couldn't breathe. The sanctuary spun. He sat down before the closing prayer, and tears spilled over without warning.

That evening, he told his wife, "*I thought I was healed. I thought I'd given it to God.*" What returned that morning wasn't just memory. It was grief. Guilt. The echo of prayers unanswered and lives lost. What returned was his moral injury, silent, buried, and now awakened by a brother in pain.

Later, in solitude, Daniel found his way to 2 Corinthians. He read Paul's strange confession: "*Three times I pleaded with the Lord about this, that it should leave me. But he said to me, 'My grace is sufficient for you, for my power is made perfect in weakness'*" (2 Corinthians 12:8-9). Something in him softened. Maybe healing didn't mean it was all gone. Maybe it meant he could live with the thorn, not as punishment, but as proof that he still cared.

Pain's return wasn't failure. It was the cost of still having a heart.

## When the Thorn Remains

We rarely talk about the persistence of pain in the Christian life. We celebrate deliverance, and rightly so, but Scripture never promises that all wounds vanish on our timeline. Like Paul, we may carry thorns in our flesh: recurring griefs, anxieties, regrets, flashbacks, or chronic trauma symptoms that God does not remove. Instead, He fills those places with grace.

The return of pain doesn't mean your healing has stalled. It may mean that God is reshaping how you define strength. It is not the absence of weakness, but the indwelling of grace. *"For when I am weak, then I am strong"* (2 Corinthians 12:10).

Sometimes, the greatest healing is not the removal of pain, but the restoration of perspective. We are not what we feel in your lowest moment. We are who God calls you in every moment: beloved.

## Restoring the Wounded Narrative

When pain returns, shame often follows close behind. *"Why am I like this? Shouldn't I be over it?"* However, that narrative, the one that tells us we're broken or disappointing, is not from God. Shame silences, but grace re-narrates.

As you face recurring pain, try telling your story differently: *"I am someone who has walked through fire, and still rises." "I am healing, not failing." "I am strong enough to feel this and still be loved." "I am not alone."*

The goal is not to escape the pain. It's to carry it with sacred tenderness and not let it own you. Healing means you are no longer running. You are facing it, eyes open, heart anchored, soul held.

## Spirit-Led Recovery

Finally, let's remember that the Spirit of God does not abandon us when trauma returns. In fact, His presence often becomes clearest in those moments. *"Likewise, the Spirit helps us in our weakness . . . the Spirit himself intercedes for us with groanings too deep for words"* (Romans 8:26). God is not waiting for you to "get it together." He is groaning with you. And where there are groans, there is also grace.

if today feels like a return to an old wound, pause and take a breath. This is not the beginning again. It's the sacred echo of a story God is still writing. We are not broken all over again; we are being met again. It's in that meeting, healing continues.

## Looking Ahead: The Gentle Work of Grace

When pain resurfaces, it often stirs up questions we thought were settled. We may find ourselves wondering if we are still lovable, if God is still near, or if healing is still possible. These are not signs of failure. They are reminders that healing is still happening and that our hearts remain tender to what matters most.

God does not grow weary of our questions. He welcomes them. He responds not with rebuke, but with presence. When Elijah was exhausted and defeated, God did not send fire or thunder. He came in a whisper. *"And after the fire the sound of a low whisper"* (1 Kings 19:12). That whisper still speaks. It says, *"You are not alone. I am with you. We will walk this together."*

There are moments when pain returns, not to punish, but to show that something deeper is being healed. These moments are not setbacks. They are invitations—back to grace, back to truth, and back to the arms of a Savior who still bears scars. And as we keep walking forward, we begin to notice something else. The pain may still visit, but it no longer speaks as loudly. Its power begins to fade, not because it has vanished, but because it is now met with the voice of Christ instead of the voice of shame.

## Reflection

Healing is not a straight line, it is a sacred spiral. As we grow stronger, our soul invites us to revisit old wounds, not to relive them, but to reclaim them with new strength and clarity. When the pain returns, it's not a failure of healing, but a furthering of it. You are being invited to tend gently to what is surfacing now with tools you didn't have before. The return of pain can become a revelation: a space where the Spirit is still at work, teaching you to trust grace again. Even when we feel like we're back at the beginning, we're not. We are further along than we know. God is not done healing what still hurts.

## Prayer

Lord Jesus, You bore scars that never disappeared, wounds that told the truth of suffering and love. When my pain returns, remind me that I am not broken again, but being invited to heal more deeply. Help me meet myself with compassion, not condemnation. Teach me to listen to what my soul and body are trying to say. Let your Spirit guide me through the spiral of healing, even when it feels like I'm circling back. Anchor me in your love when I feel unsteady, and surround me with reminders that I am not alone. Thank you for being with me in every wave of pain, every breath of peace, and every return. Amen.

## Scripture

*"The steadfast love of the Lord never ceases; his mercies never come to an end; they are new every morning; great is your faithfulness."* Lamentations 3:22-23

*"When you pass through the waters, I will be with you; and through the rivers, they shall not overwhelm you; when you walk through fire, you shall not be burned, and the flame shall not consume you."* Isaiah 43:2

## Reflection Questions

1. When was the last time pain resurfaced unexpectedly? How did you respond to it?

_____

_____

_____

_____

2.  What are some ways you can gently remind yourself "this is not then," that you are safe now?

_____

_____

_____

_____

_____

3.  Are there specific triggers we've identified that invite you into deeper healing rather than shame?

_____

_____

_____

_____

4.  How can you practice compassion toward yourself in moments of regression or emotional struggle?

_____

_____

_____

_____

5. When do triggers or flashbacks show up most in your life? What do you typically feel or experience in those moments?

_____

_____

_____

_____

_____

6. Who in your life helps you remember that healing is not a solitary journey?

_____

_____

_____

_____

_____

Chapter 15:

# WALKING WITH OTHERS IN THEIR PAIN

There comes a time in the healing journey when your story is no longer just for you. It's not that you're done healing; none of us ever fully are. But there's a quiet shift.

When we walk with others in their pain, we do so not because we have all the answers, but because we know what it feels like to have none. We show up not with solutions, but with presence. Just as Jesus did. *"Rejoice with those who rejoice, weep with those who weep."* Romans 12:15

**The pain we once thought would destroy us becomes the very ground on which we can stand beside someone else. Not as a rescuer. Not as a savior. But as a witness.**

## The Power of Presence

One of the most sacred gifts we can offer is presence. Not a solution, not an explanation, not a story meant to fix what hurts. Just the quiet strength of being there, steady, patient, and real.

In *The Bronze Scar*, I wrote, *"Helping someone with trauma is less about what you say and more about how you stay."* That still rings true. They need to know **The traumatized don't need our sermons; they need our steadiness.** that when their pain surfaces, we won't flinch or flee. Jesus modeled this beautifully. In the garden of Gethsemane, He didn't ask His disciples to fix anything. He asked them to stay awake with Him. He simply wanted companionship in His agony. *"My soul is very sorrowful, even to death; remain here, and watch with me"* (Matthew 26:38).

When someone entrusts us with their story of pain, they're not asking us to carry it; they're asking us not to walk away from it. **by staying, we take part in one of the most Christlike ministries we will ever receive: the ministry of presence.**

After the resurrection, two followers walked the road to Emmaus, burdened by grief and confusion, trying to make sense of all they had witnessed in Jerusalem. Jesus didn't arrive in a blaze of glory. He didn't begin with explanations or declarations. He simply came alongside them. *"Jesus himself drew near and went with them. But their eyes were kept from recognizing him"* (Luke 24:15-16).

This is the sacred pattern of spiritual companionship: walking alongside someone long enough for their eyes to begin to see again. Not rushing their revelation and not pushing them forward, and simply journeying with them until the fog starts to lift. Jesus listened first. Then He gently reinterpreted Scripture. Then He shared a meal. Only then were their eyes opened. Insight doesn't lead the way—presence does. When going with others through pain, their primary need is not our perspective, but our willingness to simply be present. We choose to listen instead of being direct. To remain still instead of rushing to speak. Healing unfolds in its own time, and love honors that pace.

## Bearing Burdens Without Becoming the Answer

Paul calls us to *"Bear one another's burdens, and so fulfill the law of Christ"* (Galatians 6:2). But just a few verses later, he adds: *"Each will have to bear his own load"* (v. 5).

Helping others requires balance: we are invited to walk alongside, not carry burdens for them. Trauma can tempt us into over-functioning, trying to fix or rescue. But that's not our role. Even Jesus didn't impose healing; He asked, "Do you want to be healed?" He respected the agency and readiness of every person He met.

You're not the hero in someone else's story. You're a lantern-bearer, not the light itself. We walk beside people as companions, not saviors. When we confuse the two, we burn out. But when we walk with boundaries and compassion, we create space for the Spirit to do what only God can do.

Elena hadn't spoken in group for six weeks. She showed up every time, but she sat with her arms folded, eyes down. Others shared their stories, some trembling, some tearful, and Elena stayed quiet. Until one evening, after a story that mirrored her own too closely, she whispered, *"Me too."* Her voice cracked. Her whole body shook. And no one in the circle moved to fix it. That was the miracle.

No one rushed in to stop the tears. No one flooded the space with theology or platitudes. One person simply scooted their chair closer and said, "I'm still here." That moment broke something open in Elena. And for the first time in years, she didn't feel alone inside her pain.

## Holding Space, Not Solving Stories

Walking with others doesn't mean we become their therapist, pastor, or parent. It means we learn how to hold space, to sit with another's suffering without trying to rush them through it. Holding space means:

- Listening without interrupting

- Asking before offering advice

- Respecting their pace, not imposing ours

- Praying silently as they speak, letting the Spirit lead

- Letting their pain exist without correcting it

You don't need perfect words. You need to be safe. In trauma-informed care, we say: *"People don't heal from being told what to do. They heal from being seen, heard, and believed."* That's what Jesus did again and again.

There's a sacred mystery in walking alongside someone else: in the process of offering presence, we often find healing for ourselves. This isn't about codependence or rescuing—it's about mutuality. Showing up for another person has a way of quietly reminding us of what's still true in our own story: we are not alone, not beyond redemption, not without purpose in our pain. As Paul writes, *"If one member suffers, all suffer together; if one member is honored, all rejoice together"* (1 Corinthians 12:26). This is the body of Christ—not a stage for pretending, but a fellowship where suffering and hope is shared.

When we accompany others with compassion and presence, our own story is re-lit with grace. The fragments of what survived become bridges of empathy. And sometimes, as we hold space for another, we realize that God is holding space for us too.

Marcus volunteered at a local VA hospital. Every Thursday, he made rounds, offering prayer if it was welcomed, or simply sitting beside those who didn't want to talk. One man, Sergeant D., hadn't spoken a word to him in four months. Marcus kept coming anyway. One day, Sergeant D. broke the silence. *"You don't say much,"* he said. Marcus smiled. *"Neither do you."* A pause. *"But you come back."* That simple exchange marked a beginning. Not a dramatic healing, but a connection. A signal that the presence had mattered.

In trauma ministry, showing up again and again is sometimes the most eloquent testimony of God's faithfulness. When we walk with others through pain, we offer echoes of divine consistency, love that doesn't vanish, presence that doesn't retreat.

Walking with someone through their pain holds a quiet mystery: as we offer presence, something in us begins to mend, too. This isn't rescuing, and it's not codependence. It's the grace of mutuality. In showing up for others, we often find ourselves remembering truths we've struggled to believe for ourselves. We are not alone. We are not beyond the reach of grace. We are not lost in our pain. Paul captures this beautifully: *"If one member suffers, all suffer together; if one member is honored, all rejoice together"* (1 Corinthians 12:26). This is the Church, not a stage for appearances, but a community woven together by shared sorrow and shared hope.

We are called to walk with others as God walks with us, not ahead to drag, not behind to push, but beside, hand in hand. And in that companionship, we learn to love more like Christ.

## Burnout or Compassion: Knowing the Difference

One of the greatest risks in walking with others is emotional fatigue, especially if we mistake over-involvement for compassion. Compassion leads us toward others in love; burnout pulls us into their pain without boundaries.

Jesus constantly modeled compassionate presence with limits. He withdrew to pray. He said no. He entrusted people to the Father. Following His example means learning to recognize when our "help" is actually becoming control, and when our "presence" is replacing God's role with our own.

Here are a few questions to ask yourself: *"Am I praying for them more than worrying about them? Am I trying to fix what God hasn't asked me to fix? Do I believe the Spirit is at work even when I'm not?"* Healthy compassion knows its place. It loves deeply without drowning. It stays available without being consumed.

To walk wisely with others through pain, consider these practices: offer rhythms, not reactions. Don't just show up when there's a crisis; build a consistent, relational presence. Create consent-based conversations. Ask: *"Would it help to talk about it?"* or *"Do you want me to listen or offer ideas?"* Ground yourself first. Don't enter someone else's trauma space if you're not centered in Christ yourself.

Bless the small moments. Healing doesn't always come through wisdom or words. Sometimes, it arrives through warmth. A text sent with care. A prayer offered in the stillness. A walk shared in silence. These simple gestures may seem insignificant, but they hold the weight of presence. Often, that quiet presence speaks louder than anything else.

Walking with others in their pain isn't glamorous. It's not quick. It's rarely neat. But it is holy. When you choose to stay near the hurting, you become a signpost of the kingdom: love that stays, truth that listens, and hope that doesn't demand a deadline. And in the end, this is how we will be known, not by our eloquence, but by our love. "For as much as you did it to one of the least of these . . . you did it to me." (Matthew 25:40)

## Creating Safety in the Church for Trauma Survivors

Faith communities can be places of profound healing or deep retraumatization. Many trauma survivors walk into sanctuaries hoping to find rest, only to encounter pressure, shallow theology, or silence around their pain.

To walk with trauma survivors in church settings, we must intentionally create emotionally safe spaces: Avoid demanding vulnerability from the pulpit or small groups. Train leaders in trauma-awareness, language, triggers, and signs of overwhelm. Normalize lament alongside praise. Allow grief to have a seat at the table. Make prayer and altar times voluntary, not performative or pressured. Let healing take time. Don't rush stories to their "testimony" stage.

One woman said, "*What healed me wasn't the sermon.* It was the greeter who didn't flinch when I said, "*I was divorced because of abuse.*" It was the elder who said, "*We're just glad you're here. That's when I exhaled.*" Trauma-informed churches aren't perfect. But they are safe enough for the broken to breathe. In trauma ministry, the tone is as important as the truth. And the truth, when wrapped in compassion, becomes a vessel for healing.

## When Helping Hurts: The Weight We Carry

Walking with others in their pain is a sacred calling, but it is also costly. Those who minister to the wounded often carry invisible burdens of their own. This is especially true for clergy, chaplains, healthcare workers, and counselors. We bear witness to stories others can't imagine. We hold space for emotions that linger long after the room is empty.

**The danger isn't always in doing too much. Sometimes, it's in taking on too much.**

188

What starts as compassion can quietly turn into something heavier, something harder to name. The line between empathy and entanglement begins to blur. We lose sleep over stories that aren't ours. We carry sorrow that doesn't belong to us. And somewhere along the way, we confuse God's invitation to be present with a pressure to fix, to heal, to save. Left unchecked, that weight becomes soul-deep exhaustion—the kind that no rest can cure.

Jesus Himself modeled the sacred rhythm of ministry and rest. After long days of healing and teaching, He withdrew to quiet places to pray (Luke 5:16). Rather than trying to meet every need, He embraced His human limits. Not everyone was healed. Not every town was visited. At times, He simply said no. People were entrusted to the Father's care. This rhythm of surrender and wisdom invites us to do the same.

If you are someone who walks with others, especially those carrying trauma, ask yourself: *"Who am I debriefing with? Am I making time for solitude, silence, and Sabbath? Have I mistaken burden-bearing for Messiah-complex? What signs of compassion fatigue am I ignoring?"*

Caring well for others means learning to care for yourself. Not selfishly, but wisely, sustainably, and spiritually. Your soul matters to God. And your ministry will only remain healthy if you remain whole. Let your presence be an overflow, not a depletion.

## Reflection

We don't need a platform to walk with someone in their pain. We don't need a degree, a certification, or a perfect track record. What we need is courage, compassion, and the willingness to stay when others might walk away. Walking with someone through trauma is holy ground. We may never be thanked. We may never see the fruit. But in showing up with love and not flinching when the wound appears, you mirror Christ Himself. This is the ministry of staying. And in it, we bear one another's burdens, not to save, but to stand.

## Prayer

Jesus, You never rushed the hurting. You walked roads with them. You sat in silence. You asked questions. You wept. Teach me to do the same. When someone around me is in pain, help me resist the urge to fix and instead offer presence. Make me a safe place for others, someone who listens more than speaks, waits more than pushes, and loves without condition. Let my own scars become reminders that You still heal, and that You walk with us through the valley, not just on the mountaintop. And when I grow weary, remind me that You never ask me to carry what only You can hold. Thank You for walking with me. Teach me now to walk with others. Amen.

## Scripture

*"Rejoice with those who rejoice, weep with those who weep."* Romans 12:15

*"Bear one another's burdens, and so fulfill the law of Christ."* Galatians 6:2

*"Each will have to bear his own load."* Galatians 6:5

*"If one member suffers, all suffer together; if one member is honored, all rejoice together."* 1 Corinthians 12:26

## Reflection Questions

1. When have you felt the healing presence of someone simply staying with you in your pain?

---

---

---

---

2. What are your greatest fears or hesitations in walking with someone through trauma?

---

---

---

---

3. How can you ensure you're supporting without over-functioning or rescuing?

_____

_____

_____

_____

_____

4. Which Scripture in this chapter speaks most deeply to your experience of presence and healing?

_____

_____

_____

_____

_____

5. What would it look like to embody the ministry of staying this week?

_____

_____

_____

_____

Chapter 16

# THE POWER OF PRESENCE: WHAT MAKES HEALING POSSIBLE

Some wounds run too deep for words. No explanation can untangle the ache, and even the kindest advice can fall short. In those sacred spaces of grief, trauma, or unspeakable loss, what matters most is not a solution, but a person. It's not about what is said, but about who is willing to stay. Presence becomes the ointment words cannot offer. It's a quiet strength that holds space when everything else feels like too much.

I've lived this truth. In my own darkest moments, what helped most wasn't the right phrase or some polished encouragement. It was the people who showed up and stayed. I can't recall exactly what they said, but I remember that they were there. Their presence carved a path toward healing that no lecture ever could. The ones who simply sat with me, prayed beside me, or waited in silence left a mark deeper than any words. They reminded me I wasn't alone. And that reminder changed everything.

## Presence is the language of healing

Long before trauma theory caught up with it, Scripture revealed a truth that resonates in the deepest places of our pain. God does not abandon us in suffering. He moves *closer*. In Jesus, God entered our pain, not merely to observe it, but to *bear it with us*. This is the foundation of all true ministry to those who suffer: the willingness to show up, stay near, and offer the healing gift of presence.

There's something profoundly spiritual about simply being there. When Job's friends first arrived after his life was shattered, their greatest act of compassion was not their theology, but their silence: "*They sat with him on the ground seven days and seven nights, and no one spoke a word to him, for they saw that his suffering was very great*" (Job 2:13). Their later speeches would be full of misplaced assumptions, but in those early moments, they got one thing right. They stayed.

In trauma recovery, presence is more than proximity. It's an active, compassionate availability that communicates: *We are not alone in this*. It does not try to control or rush the healing process. It does not try to fix. It simply remains, and that is often enough to create the space where healing can begin.

When someone is in the aftermath of trauma, their internal world feels shattered. The brain, flooded with stress hormones, loses its sense of time, place, and safety. Survivors often feel disconnected not only from others but from themselves. Their nervous systems are on high alert, expecting danger around every corner. What restores safety isn't a lecture. It's not even a perfect plan. It's a person.

Presence is a deeply embodied signal to the brain and heart: *You are safe now.* When someone sits beside us without judgment, listens without needing to fix anything, and stays without fleeing from our pain, their very presence becomes an anchor. It activates the parasympathetic nervous system, slowing the heart rate, deepening the breath, and helping the body return to a state of calm after hypervigilance. From a trauma-informed lens, this is called "co-regulation", when the calm of one person helps stabilize the storm in another. However, what secular psychology refers to as co-regulation, we also recognize as incarnational ministry.

In the person of Jesus, God did not remain distant from human suffering. He stepped into our trauma. He stepped into the blood and the dirt, the betrayal and the fear, the injustice and the loss. His presence was not merely symbolic; it carried redemptive power. And that same presence, now mediated through His Spirit and through His people, becomes a lifeline for those who feel like they are drowning in pain. In the person of Jesus, God did not remain distant from human suffering. He stepped into our trauma, into the blood and the dirt, the betrayal and the fear, the injustice, and the loss. He was "a man of sorrows and acquainted with grief" (Isaiah 53:3). His presence wasn't merely symbolic; it had redemptive power. And it is this same presence, now mediated through His Spirit and His people, that becomes the lifeline for those drowning in pain.

Showing up with compassion reflects the very heart of Christ. Sitting quietly with someone in their pain mirrors what He did in Gethsemane, staying near even when words had run out. When we choose not to look away, we take part in the ministry Jesus modeled. It is a presence that does not fix, but faithfully remains.

I remember sitting in a dimly lit room at a military hospital overseas. The walls were thin. The silence inside was not peace; it was the absence of what had once been a vibrant life. A young Airman, barely twenty-two, had taken his own life after a long, invisible battle. His commander stood near the doorway, staring at the floor, and wringing his hands. No words. Just questions that had no answer.

The mother arrived that night. Her son had been gone for hours. She knew it. But when I met her at the hospital entrance, she didn't want a speech. She didn't want a Scripture. She wanted to sit beside her son. I didn't offer a theological explanation. I simply walked with her to the room. I sat with her in silence for a long time, praying in my spirit but saying nothing aloud. She clutched his jacket. She wept. And I stayed.

In that moment, nothing I could have said would have brought peace. But my presence meant she didn't have to walk through that valley alone. Later, she told me something I'll never forget: "*You didn't talk over my grief. You sat in it with me. That's the only thing that helped.*" That's the power of presence. It's not heroic. It's not about the right words or the perfect prayer. It's about staying close. When trauma hollows out a person's world, your presence becomes a bridge to hope.

This is something every trauma-informed caregiver must embrace. The ministry of presence is not a passive resignation; it is a sacred offering. A calm, grounded presence becomes the means through which someone relearns that not every moment of vulnerability will be met with abandonment or harm.

## God's Nearness in Our Pain

The healing power of presence is not a human invention. It reflects something essential about who God is. Scripture does not present a distant deity who merely observes suffering from a cosmic perch. Instead, we see a God who draws near.

*"Fear not, for I am with you; be not dismayed, for I am your God; I will strengthen you, I will help you, I will uphold you with my righteous right hand"* (Isaiah 41:10). Time and time again, God responds to pain not with explanations, but with Himself.

When Jesus told His disciples, *"I am with you always, to the end of the age"* (Matthew 28:20), He wasn't offering a metaphor. He was promising a presence that would sustain them through persecution, fear, grief, and loss. His Spirit would inhabit every lonely place they walked. That promise remains today. It is the heartbeat of Christian ministry.

We saw this in Emma's story. After surviving sexual assault, she withdrew into herself, afraid to trust, unsure if anyone could really understand. But it wasn't just trauma support groups or theological ideas that began to heal her. It was presence. Someone sat with her, cried with her, and prayed when she couldn't. Slowly, the truth of God's nearness became real, not just as a verse, but as a *felt reality*. And that, more than anything, allowed her to begin trusting again.

This is why presence matters: it is how people experience the nearness of God. Offering presence doesn't mean you have to have all the answers. In fact, it often means resisting the urge to give them. Presence is not about fixing; it's about *faithfully remaining*.

Presence is not passive; it is a powerful, intentional ministry that reflects the heart of God. For those walking alongside someone who has experienced trauma, here are five essential truths that shape a faithful, healing presence:

## 1. Show Up, Even When It's Awkward

Presence begins with proximity. One of the deepest wounds trauma inflicts is the feeling of abandonment, of being left alone in the dark. That's why simply showing up, even if you feel unsure of what to do or say, is one of the most meaningful gifts you can offer.

You don't have to arrive with a sermon. Your ministry begins the moment you arrive and sit down. Awkwardness is not a barrier; it's a sign that you care enough to step into sacred territory without trying to control it. It's okay to say, *"I don't know what to say, but I didn't want you to be alone."* That honesty can bring more healing than a polished speech. The power is in your presence, not your performance.

## 2. Listen Without Rushing the Story

Trauma survivors often need to reclaim their voice. Telling their story, on their terms, in their timing, is part of that process. Your role is not to direct or hurry the narrative, but to hold space for it. This means letting the silence linger when needed. It means resisting the temptation to fill in the blanks or interpret what they're saying. Sometimes, survivors will repeat themselves or revisit the same memories; this isn't a lack of progress, but rather a natural process by which the mind and heart begin to make sense of what happened.

Give them the gift of time and patience. Listening deeply is one of the rarest and most healing acts of love.

## 3. Don't Reach for Platitudes

When people are in pain, especially the raw, soul-level pain of trauma, they're not usually looking for answers; they're looking for understanding. Yet, in our discomfort, we often reach for religious clichés that feel safe and familiar:

- *"Everything happens for a reason."*

- *"God won't give you more than you can handle."*

- *"At least it wasn't worse."*

- *"They're in a better place."*

While these phrases may be well-intentioned, they often come across as dismissive or even harmful. They shortcut the grieving process, minimize the depth of someone's pain, and suggest that there is something wrong with feeling devastated. In trauma care, such statements can compound shame and isolation.

People need the freedom to hurt without having their hurt "explained away." Platitudes often function as a way for us to feel better, not the person suffering. They relieve our discomfort more than they meet the other person's needs.

Instead, trauma-informed presence says:

- *"I'm so sorry this happened to you."*

- *"I don't have answers, but I'm here."*

- *"That sounds incredibly painful. I can't imagine."*

- *"I'm not going anywhere."*

Presence is about making space for truth, not offering quick answers to dull its sting. It requires the humility to stay close without trying to control or tidy someone's grief. In doing so, we become witnesses to their pain, not a judge or a fixer. That's when people begin to feel seen, safe, and, eventually, ready to heal.

## 4. Stay the Course

Healing doesn't follow a schedule. Trauma recovery often unfolds in waves, progress followed by setbacks, moments of hope followed by fresh grief. The people who make the deepest impact are not those who rush in with energy during the crisis, but those who stay long after the casseroles are gone and the texts have stopped coming.

Staying the course means showing up weeks, months, even years later. It means remembering anniversaries, checking in on quiet days, and offering your presence even when the trauma no longer dominates every conversation. Sometimes, the most healing words are: *"I'm still here."*

Faithfulness builds safety. Safety builds trust. And trust opens the door to healing.

## 5. Stay Grounded in God

Walking with someone in their pain can stir your own. You may feel helpless, overwhelmed, or even triggered. That's why caregivers must stay rooted, not in their own strength, but in God's. Jesus often withdrew to pray, not because He lacked compassion, but because He knew the source of His strength. You must do the same. Let God refill you so you can pour out His peace, not just your emotional reserves.

Being grounded also means recognizing your role: you are not the Savior. You are not the Healer. You are not responsible for their transformation. Your job is to love, to reflect the nearness of Christ, and to trust the Holy Spirit to do what only He can.

## Reflection Remaining When Others Leave

There's something sacred about the presence of someone who simply refuses to leave. When trauma leaves us shattered and uncertain, a steady companion becomes a vessel of God's grace. They remind us, often without words, that we are not forgotten, not too broken, not too much to bear.

Presence doesn't solve the mystery of suffering, but it reflects the heart of God, who draws near to us in our pain and stays. The greatest gift we can offer to those walking through trauma is not our wisdom, but our willingness to stay. Even in your own healing, this is true. God is not rushing you, lecturing you, or shaming you for how long it's taking. He is *with you*, faithfully, patiently, lovingly present.

## Prayer

Lord, You are near to the brokenhearted and present in every valley of pain. Help me to remember that healing often begins not with answers, but with presence. Teach me to be a companion who listens more than I speak, who stays even when it's hard, and who reflects Your faithful love in how I show up. For those walking through the shadows, let them feel Your nearness through the presence of others, and through mine. In Jesus' name, Amen.

## Scripture

*"The Lord is near to the brokenhearted and saves the crushed in spirit."* Psalm 34:18

## Reflection Questions

1. When has someone's presence made a difference in your life during a painful season?

2. Why do you think silence and presence can be more powerful than words?

_____

_____

_____

_____

_____

3. What makes it hard to offer presence to someone who is suffering?

_____

_____

_____

_____

_____

4. How do you care for your own soul while walking with others through trauma?

_____

_____

_____

_____

5. In what ways can you reflect God's nearness to someone in your life
   right now?

_____

_____

_____

_____

_____

Chapter 17:

# REBUILDING TRUST IN GOD AFTER TRAUMA

Trauma doesn't just break the heart; it breaks the bridge between hearts. It fractures trust: trust in people, trust in institutions, trust in one's own judgment, and sometimes, trust in God. For the survivor, the most pressing question after trauma is no longer *Why did this happen?* but *"Who can I trust now?"* And more deeply still, *"Can I ever trust again?"*

This is the landscape many trauma survivors live in, not denial, not even despair, but chronic vigilance. Hyper-awareness. A soul that's been singed and now flinches at warmth. We don't call that weakness. We call it wisdom forged in fire.

Rebuilding trust is sacred work. It cannot be forced or rushed. It's not about forgetting what happened; it's about finding our footing again in a world where the floor once gave way. And it requires more than platitudes. It requires presence.

Trust, once broken, cannot be easily restored. It must be rebuilt, brick by brick, breath by breath, not with promises but with proof. For trauma survivors, trust feels like a bridge suspended over a canyon. Every step is a risk. Every step requires courage. And what helps most is not someone shouting from the other side, it's someone willing to walk back across and meet you in the middle.

God does exactly that. He never demands blind faith from the broken. Instead, He draws near. From Genesis to Revelation, God shows Himself as One who walks with the wounded. He meets Hagar in the desert. Elijah under the broom tree. Jesus, the wounded Healer, enters locked rooms and begins again with the very ones who fled. This is not the God of pressure. This is the God of presence.

Kayla grew up in church. Her father led the men's ministry. Her mother led the women's Bible study. On Sundays, they looked like the perfect family. But behind the stained-glass smiles were power plays, silence as punishment, and Scripture used as a weapon.

She learned that trust could be leveraged. That love could be taken away. That even faith could be faked. By her twenties, Kayla had stopped praying, not because she didn't believe in God, but because she didn't believe He was safe. "*I figured if He was anything like my father, I was better off without Him.*" When she came to the trauma recovery group, she sat in silence. Arms folded. Eyes scanning. Always near the door.

In the third session, she spoke. Barely above a whisper. "*I told God this was His last chance.*" No one pounced. No one handed her a verse. No one promised her healing in a timeline. We just stayed. Week by week, her voice grew stronger.

She started asking questions, not apologetic debates, but honest ones: *"How do you know someone is safe?"* *"Does God get tired of hearing the same thing?"* Months passed. And one night, after everyone else had left, she lingered behind. She said, *"I still don't trust easily. But I'm starting to believe that maybe . . . maybe God didn't walk away."* That's the miracle. Trust doesn't return in a rush; it returns in fragments. In silence. In the presence of those who don't run.

## A Theology of Trust: The God Who Stays

Trust is a spiritual issue, not just a psychological one. It is foundational to how we relate to God, others, and even ourselves. When trauma occurs, especially at the hands of someone who held power or claimed spiritual authority, the rupture in trust cuts deep into the soul. It's not just a question of *"Can I be safe again?"* but *"Can I believe again?"* And underneath it all: *"Can I trust God?"* The Gospel answers that question, not with a lecture, but with a Person.

Throughout Scripture, trust is forged not in moments of ease but in seasons of deep distress. God reveals Himself not as the One who fixes pain instantly, but as the One who enters it. His trustworthiness is not proven by our escape from hardship, but by His enduring presence within it. *"The Lord is near to the brokenhearted and saves the crushed in spirit"* (Psalm 34:18).

This nearness is covenantal. From the beginning, God has bound Himself to His people with the language of loyalty: *"I will be their God, and they shall be my people"* (Jeremiah 31:33). These are not just words; they are vows. And unlike human promises, God's covenant is never broken.

When Adam and Eve hid, God came looking. When Hagar ran, God followed and gave her the name El Roi, the God who sees. When Elijah collapsed beneath the weight of despair, God sent an angel, not with commands, but with a nap and a meal. And when humanity was crushed under sin and death, God did not shout from heaven. He came down. In Jesus Christ, God became the vulnerable one. He entered trauma. He lived it. He bore betrayal, abandonment, injustice, violence, and death. And in His resurrection, He showed that trust, though shattered, can be raised again.

This is the God who stays. When others walk away, He remains. When trust feels fragile and faith is threadbare, He does not leave. Even when we no longer have the strength to seek Him, He is near. His faithfulness doesn't depend on our grip, but on His unshakable hold on us. *"If we are faithless, He remains faithful—for He cannot deny Himself"* (2 Timothy 2:13).

To trust again, we have to unlearn the lie that God resembles those who hurt us. He doesn't wound to control. He doesn't manipulate or withdraw. His presence isn't a threat—it's a refuge. Steady and kind, He stays close. And even when all we can manage is a shaky breath in His direction, that's enough. He matches our pace, walking with us—patient, present, and endlessly gentle.

## What Rebuilding Trust Requires:

## 1. Trust Is Rebuilt Through Consistency.

The traumatized brain is always watching. It scans for danger, notices patterns, and memorizes disappointment. For survivors, one missed call, one abrupt shift in tone, one forgotten promise can reinforce the idea: No one is safe. This is why consistency matters more than intensity. Small, repeated acts of kindness rebuild the architecture of safety. Someone who shows up again and again, without demand or judgment, becomes a living message: I'm still here. You're still safe.

This is how God reveals Himself: not through dramatic spectacle, but through steadfast presence. *"The steadfast love of the Lord never ceases; his mercies never come to an end"* (Lamentations 3:22). Steadfastness is love that refuses to walk away. We often expect healing to come from dramatic breakthroughs. But most of the time, trust is rebuilt over coffee, through check-ins, in a gentle tone, in remembered birthdays, in silent rooms where someone simply stays.

## 2. Trust Is Rebuilt through Safety

Safety is more than physical protection; it is emotional protection. Safe people don't force disclosure. They don't shame silence. They don't weaponize prayer or Scripture. They respect boundaries and honor pacing.

Jesus was the safest Person to ever walk the earth. And yet He never coerced. When the hemorrhaging woman touched His robe, He didn't scold, He restored. When Thomas doubted, Jesus didn't withdraw; He extended His wounds. Safe people make space for you to be who you are. This is why survivors don't need spiritual pressure; they need presence. They don't need solutions; they need someone who says, *"You don't have to explain everything. I'm here."*

## 3. Trust Is Rebuilt through Time

There is no timetable for restoration. When someone has experienced betrayal, trauma, or abandonment, their sense of time distorts. The clock doesn't move at the same pace for a hurting heart. That's why the most healing words are not *"You should be over this,"* but *"Take the time you need."* God understands this. *"He remembers that we are dust"* (Psalm 103:14). He does not rush or scold. He never demands speed.

If you're learning to trust again, give yourself grace for how long it takes. And if you're walking with someone in pain, resist the urge to "fix." Trust is not rebuilt in the fast lane. It's built on the long, slow road of grace.

## 4. Trust Is Rebuilt through Community

Trauma thrives in isolation. Healing requires connection. Not crowds. Not pressure. But communion, spaces where someone can show up as they are, and be received with gentleness. *"Bear one another's burdens, and so fulfill the law of Christ* (Galatians 6:2). We were never meant to carry pain alone. Real community reflects the heart of God: it stays. It listens. It remembers. And when trust falters, it lends faith until faith returns. Community doesn't demand. It makes room. And in that room, trust can begin to breathe again.

## 5. Trust Is Anchored in God's Nature

All human beings, even the best among us, will fail at some point. That's why our ultimate anchor cannot be in people alone. It must be in the unchanging character of God. *"Jesus Christ is the same yesterday and today and forever"* (Hebrews 13:8). When everything else shakes, He does not. He does not shift with moods. He does not walk away when we're struggling. His nature is not dependent on our performance. He is faithful when we are unsure. He is present when we are anxious. He is strong when we feel undone. To rebuild trust, we must re-anchor our hearts in the One who never fails.

## Reflection

Rebuilding trust after trauma is like stitching torn fabric with trembling hands. Every thread matters. Every knot of courage counts. There is no need to rush. The pressure to "get over it" is the voice of the world, not the voice of Christ. Jesus never rushed the grieving. He never rebuked the doubter. He invited the weary to rest. So, if all you can do today is whisper, *"Maybe I'll try again,"* that's enough.

Trust doesn't return like a lightning strike; it returns like morning. Quiet. Steady. Often unnoticed until suddenly, light is there again. The old wounds still exist, but warmth touches them differently now. And when you begin to trust again, even a little, you'll find that God was there all along. Not demanding but waiting. Not watching from afar, but sitting quietly beside you, weaving healing into the places you thought would stay torn forever.

*You don't have to leap. Just lean.

*You don't have to be ready. Just be willing.

*You don't have to be whole. Just be held.

## Prayer

God, You know where trust was broken in me. You know the faces of those who hurt me, the places where my heart learned to flinch, the memories I carry without asking for them. I want to trust again, but I need You to be patient with me. Thank You that You are steady, not volatile. Safe, not forceful. Present, not punishing. Walk with me as I take one small step at a time. Heal what I no longer have words for. Help me not only to find trustworthy people, but to become one myself. And most of all, help me remember that You have never left. In Jesus' name, Amen.

## Scripture

*"Those who know your name put their trust in you, for you, O Lord, have not forsaken those who seek you."* Psalm 9:10

## Reflection Questions

1. What did trust mean to you before your trauma, and how has that changed?

_____

_____

_____

2. Which of the five rebuilding truths speaks to your current season of healing?

_____

_____

_____

_____

3. In what specific area of life do you feel God inviting you to risk trust again?

_____

_____

_____

_____

4. In what ways can you reflect God's trustworthiness to someone else?

_____

_____

_____

_____

Chapter 18:

# WHEN FORGIVENESS FEELS IMPOSSIBLE

Forgiveness is one of the most profound and most misunderstood realities of the Christian faith. For those who have endured trauma, the very word can stir a storm of emotions: resistance, sorrow, anger, guilt, or confusion. It's not uncommon to hear phrases like, *"I know I should forgive, but I just can't,"* or *"If I forgive, am I saying what they did was, okay?"* These are not the protests of the unfaithful. They are the cries of the wounded.

Trauma changes the landscape of the heart. It teaches us to build walls to survive, to protect ourselves from further injury. And when someone wounds us, especially if they were trusted or close, forgiveness can feel like a betrayal of our pain. It can feel like letting the offender off the hook, or worse, allowing them access to wound us again. But Biblical forgiveness is not permissiveness. It is not forgetting. And it certainly is not excusing evil.

Jesus' command to forgive is not flippant or detached. When He said, *"Father, forgive them, for they know not what they do"* (Luke 23:34), He was hanging from a cross, brutalized by those He came to save. Forgiveness did not erase His wounds. It revealed His heart. And in that moment, He gave us a glimpse of the kind of forgiveness that only flows from the deepest wells of love and divine strength.

## The Wounds That Make Forgiveness Hard

Forgiveness feels impossible when the wound is still bleeding. For many trauma survivors, that wound is not in the past. It is present, throbbing in memory, emotions, and even the body. Neuroscience tells us that trauma is stored somatically. So, when we hear a voice, smell a scent, or encounter a similar situation, the brain can fire off danger signals as if the event is happening again. In that space, forgiveness feels absurd. Survival feels more urgent than sanctification.

Healing and forgiveness are not enemies. They are thoroughly intertwined. Forgiveness is not always the first step. Sometimes, healing must begin with safety, truth-telling, and grief. Only when we have had permission to feel the full weight of what was done can we even begin to consider forgiveness. And even then, forgiveness may come in layers.

**Forgiveness is rarely a one-time event.** It is more like peeling an onion, layer by layer, with each new season of healing revealing another piece that needs to be released. Sometimes we think we have forgiven, only to discover months or years later that a new memory has surfaced, and we must revisit that sacred space of surrender once again. This is not failure. This is faithfulness in the process.

There is also the deep fear that if we forgive, we are invalidating the pain. But forgiveness is not saying what happened was okay. It is saying we will not let what happened continue to rule our lives. Forgiveness is not about the offender's worthiness. It is about our own healing. We forgive because we refuse to carry the poison of resentment into our future.

## The Misconception of "Forgive and Forget"

One of the most commonly repeated phrases, "forgive and forget," often creates unnecessary confusion and guilt for trauma survivors. People will say, "I can forgive, but I'll never forget," as if forgetting is a condition for genuine forgiveness. But the deeper truth is this: we forgive not to forget, but to remember in a way that no longer controls us.

You can forgive to the point that the memory no longer holds sway over your words, your thoughts, or your relationships. That doesn't mean the event is erased from your mind. It means that the memory has been placed behind you, not because it has vanished, but because it no longer drives you.

Sometimes we believe that remembering a painful experience means we haven't truly forgiven. But in truth, the burden of carrying that memory is often part of the sacrifice we make in forgiving. The more important question is not, *"Do I still remember?"* but *"Does it still affect how I speak, think, and act toward others, especially in ways that harm trust or block healing?"*

Also, the idea of forgiveness affecting relationships isn't limited to a personal relationship with the offender. Much of the trauma we endure comes from individuals with whom we no longer, or never did, have an ongoing relationship. Forgiveness, in these cases, is about how the memory shapes your current relationships with others, with yourself, and with God. We should reclaim the phrase, not as "forgive and forget" as an unrealistic erasure, but as "forgive and forget to the point where we can put it behind us."

## When Forgiveness Is Delayed

There are times when forgiveness just doesn't come. The heart resists. The soul aches. And the burden of forgiveness feels too heavy to lift. In these moments, it is easy to believe we are failing spiritually. But delayed forgiveness is not a lack of faith—it is a sign of our humanity. God never shames us for not being ready. He invites us to be honest about where we are.

Jesus never said forgiveness would be easy. But He did promise His Spirit would help us. The journey may be slow, but slowness is not a sign of disobedience. It is often reverence. When we delay forgiveness because we are seeking to acknowledge the depth of our pain, that too, can be sacred space. What matters is that we stay open to the possibility of healing, even if we are not there yet.

We can pray, "*God, I am not ready to forgive. But I am willing to let You work on my heart.*" That prayer, however small, is a mustard seed—and God honors it.

## Sanctuaries or Scars: How the Church Handles Anger and Hurt

Carla had served in her church for more than a decade. She taught children's Sunday school, led women's Bible studies, and supported the pastoral staff with quiet faithfulness. But after raising concerns about mishandled funds and the silencing of a fellow church member's abuse disclosure, she found herself suddenly removed from leadership. Rumors spread. Friends stopped calling. The pastor's final words to her in a tense meeting were, "You need to forgive us and move on, for the sake of unity."

That phrase haunted her. It wasn't a request; it was a command laced with shame. Forgiveness, in that moment, was not an act of grace but a muzzle. What followed was a long season of disillusionment, spiritual confusion, and grief. Carla stopped attending church altogether for several months.

In therapy and through personal prayer, she began to separate God's character from the church's failings. She wrestled deeply with questions about justice, truth, and trust. Only when she was no longer pressured to forgive on someone else's timeline did she begin to rediscover what forgiveness actually was. Slowly, forgiveness became less about letting people off the hook and more about releasing her own soul from spiritual captivity.

Many people walk away from the church because the command to forgive is used against them as a weapon. True pastoral care never rushes someone through the process of forgiveness. Instead, it honors the honesty of their lament, respects their boundaries, and gently goes with them as they walk toward healing. The church should be the safest place for pain to be named and processed, not the place where pain is silenced to preserve appearances.

## Forgiveness Is Not Reconciliation

One of the most helpful distinctions for trauma survivors is the difference between forgiveness and reconciliation. Forgiveness is a one-person decision. It's an inner posture, a surrender to God's justice. Reconciliation, on the other hand, requires repentance and change from the offender, and it may never be safe or appropriate. Forgiveness: It's possible to forgive someone while still maintaining boundaries. We can forgive and still press charges, and we can forgive and never see them again.

Forgiveness doesn't mean trusting someone who has proven untrustworthy. It does not mean subjecting yourself to abuse in the name of piety. Forgiveness is not about enabling the other person—it's about freeing yourself. As Paul writes, "*Beloved, never avenge yourselves, but leave it to the wrath of God*" (Romans 12:19). Forgiveness entrusts justice to the hands of the only One fully capable of administering it.

## The Role of Lament

One of the forgotten companions of forgiveness is lament. The Psalms are full of honest cries, accusations, anger, grief, and pleas for God to act. Lament gives us language to name the evil, mourn the loss, and protest the injustice. Without lament, forgiveness can become a shallow performance. But with lament, forgiveness becomes rooted in truth. Only when we name the wound can we begin to release it.

Lament also keeps us honest with God. It invites us to say what we're really feeling, not what we think we should feel. In lament, we discover that God doesn't flinch at our rage or sorrow. He meets us in it. And from that meeting place, the journey toward forgiveness becomes possible.

Lament is not weakness; it's courage. It takes strength to admit the depth of the hurt. When we read the cries of David, Jeremiah, or Job, we don't find shallow faith. We find bold, raw trust—the kind of trust that believes God can handle our honesty. Forgiveness born in that place is durable. It is not pretense. It is truth wrapped in grace.

## Forgiving Ourselves

Sometimes the hardest person to forgive is the one in the mirror. Survivors of trauma often carry shame, not just for what happened, but for how they responded. There may be guilt for not speaking up sooner, for not seeing the signs, or for the ways the trauma changed their relationships. In some cases, there is moral injury: the pain of having violated one's own values under duress.

It's about holding them in the light of grace. The cross of Christ covers not only the sins committed against us, but the sins we carry ourselves. Paul reminds us, *"There is therefore now no condemnation for those who are in Christ Jesus"* (Romans 8:1). To forgive ourselves is not to excuse everything we've done, but to align with God's verdict of mercy.

> **Self-forgiveness is not about minimizing our mistakes; it's about accepting them.**

We must learn to speak to ourselves the way Christ speaks to us: with truth, yes, but also with tenderness. Shame has no place in the heart that Christ has made new. Forgiving ourselves is part of stepping out of shame's shadow and into the healing light of God's love.

This is often the most overlooked dimension of trauma recovery. We can spend years trying to forgive others, without ever realizing we're still holding ourselves hostage. But the mercy of God is not fragmented. It doesn't apply only to others; it reaches into our own hearts as well. When we say yes to forgiving ourselves, we are not being arrogant. We are being obedient to grace.

## Forgiveness at the Cross

Nowhere is forgiveness more mysterious, or more powerful, than in the words of Christ on the cross: *"Father, forgive them, for they know not what they do"* (Luke 23:34). He spoke those words not from a distance, but from agony. He offered forgiveness in real time, while bloodied, mocked, and pierced.

That moment is not just theological. It is deeply personal. Jesus did not wait until the resurrection to offer grace. He gave it while still being crucified. For trauma survivors, this matters. It tells us that forgiveness is not something we must wait to give until we feel whole again. Sometimes it is born right in the center of pain, not as an obligation, but as a liberation.

And we must not forget: His forgiveness did not prevent death. It did not cancel the consequence. Some would still reject Him. But for those who received it, His forgiveness became the doorway to eternal life. When we forgive, we take part in that same mystery. We open a door that no one else can shut, because Christ has already walked through it ahead of us.

Forgiveness at the cross was not clean, easy, or tidy. It was blood-soaked, heart-wrenching, and real. That means our own forgiveness journey doesn't have to be polished either. It can be messy. It can be slow. But it can also be holy.

## Reflection

Forgiveness is not the enemy of justice; it's the companion of healing and may take time. It may take years. But it is possible. And in the hands of a loving God, it becomes a gateway to freedom, not a denial of your pain. Every act of forgiveness echoes the mercy of Christ. Every step toward release breaks another link in the chain.

We don't have to feel ready. We don't even have to feel willing. What matters is being honest with God about where we truly are. From that place of truth, He meets us and gently begins to lead us toward the freedom our souls were created to know.

## Prayer

Lord, you know how deeply someone wounded me. You also know how hard it is to even think about forgiveness. Help me bring my hurt to You honestly. Teach me to lament, to grieve, and to trust You with justice. When I am ready, give me the grace to forgive—not because it's easy, but because You are with me. And because I want to be free. Amen.

## Scripture

*"Father, forgive them, for they know not what they do."* (Luke 23:34)

*"Beloved, never avenge yourselves, but leave it to the wrath of God."* (Romans 12:19)

*"Forgiving one another, as God in Christ forgave you."* (Ephesians 4:32)

*"There is therefore now no condemnation for those who are in Christ Jesus."* (Romans 8:1)

## Reflection Questions

1.  What emotions surface for you when you think about forgiveness?

---

---

---

---

2.  What has made forgiveness feel impossible on your journey?

---

---

---

---

3. How does distinguishing forgiveness from reconciliation help you?

_____

_____

_____

_____

_____

4. Who can walk with you as you explore forgiveness, gently and safely?

_____

_____

_____

_____

_____

5. What would it mean to invite God into the impossibility of forgiveness today?

_____

_____

_____

_____

_____

Chapter 19:
# RECLAIMING THE PRESENT

Healing from trauma often involves a long and painful process of moving beyond what has been lost. But for many survivors, the greatest challenge is not simply escaping the past; it's learning to reclaim the present. Trauma can lock a person in a cycle of re-experiencing, avoidance, and hypervigilance, making it difficult to inhabit the here and now with any sense of peace or purpose. As one survivor shared, *"I knew I wasn't in danger anymore, but my body didn't believe it. I was still flinching at shadows, still waiting for the other shoe to drop."*

Reclaiming the present is both a spiritual and psychological act. It is about stepping out of survival mode and beginning to live again with purpose, delight, and presence. In trauma recovery, this step often marks a major turning point. It means we're not only surviving what happened, we're learning to live again.

## The Cost of Disconnection

Trauma pulls us away from the present. Whether we're lost in flashbacks, stuck in numbing routines, or emotionally disengaged from our surroundings, our awareness becomes fragmented. This disconnection is a defense mechanism, often necessary at the time of trauma. But over time, it becomes a prison. People may find themselves going through the motions of life, unable to enjoy family, relationships, work, or even prayer. The mind may wander back to the moment of impact, or ahead to imagined disasters, but rarely settles in the present.

One man described how he used to come home from work and sit in his car for twenty minutes, unable to enter the house where his children waited. *"It wasn't that I didn't love them. I just couldn't be there. My body was with them, but my soul was stuck somewhere else."*

**Disconnection affects every dimension of life.** A survivor may attend church but feel distant during worship. Another may stop praying, not out of rebellion, but because they feel unheard. Still others may avoid friendships, worried that if someone got close, they'd see the brokenness inside. Trauma trains us to numb, to hide, to disappear.

Theologically, this disconnection has profound implications. God exists in the eternal now. In Exodus 3, when Moses asks for God's name, the Lord replies, *"I AM who I AM,* "a declaration of presence. He is not "I was" or "I will be." He is the God of the now. When we are disconnected from the present, we miss His nearness. We may pray, but feel unheard. We may worship, but feel numb. We may serve others, but feel hollow.

Jesus was called Immanuel, "God with us," not just in theory, but in time and space. His ministry was rooted in presence, in stopping, listening, touching, and noticing. To walk with Him again, we must learn to be present, too.

## Reorienting the Body and Mind

The body remembers what the mind tries to forget. Chronic muscle tension, a racing heartbeat, shallow breathing, and startle responses can keep us locked in a state of survival mode. Even when the danger is long gone, the body often hasn't received that message.

Reorienting the body begins with gentleness. Sitting quietly before God and simply noticing the body's state, tight jaw, clenched fists, shallow chest, can be a starting place. We don't fight the body; we listen to it. In that listening, we invite the Holy Spirit to bring awareness and peace.

One veteran shared how he began silently praying Psalm 46:10, *"Be still, and know that I am God,"* while walking slowly in his backyard. *"At first it felt like nothing,"* he said. *"But after a while, I realized I wasn't walking to escape, I was walking to arrive. And God was walking with me."*

The mind must also be gently retrained. Trauma distorts how we think about ourselves, others, and God. Thoughts like *"I'm not safe," "I'm broken,"* or *"God has abandoned me"* often run on autopilot. But Scripture reminds us: *"We destroy arguments and every lofty opinion raised against the knowledge of God, and take every thought captive to obey Christ"* (2 Corinthians 10:5).

This is not just an intellectual exercise. It's a spiritual discipline. Reclaiming the mind is a process of identifying lies and replacing them with God's truth. Where trauma says, *"You are alone,"* God says, *"I will never leave you"* (Hebrews 13:5). Where fear says, *"This will never change,"* God says, *"I am making all things new"* (Revelation 21:5). This shift is not always fast, but it is deeply transformative. Romans 12:2 urges us to *"be transformed by the renewal of our minds."*

This isn't just about changing opinions; it's about allowing the Spirit of God to reshape our entire way of seeing the world and ourselves.

## The Present As Sacred Ground

In Exodus 3, when Moses encounters the burning bush, God says, *"Take off your sandals, for the place where you are standing is holy ground."* This moment wasn't in a temple. It was in the wilderness. God sanctified the space not because of its setting, but because of His presence.

This has profound meaning for survivors. The present moment may not feel holy. It may feel painful, slow, or insignificant. But when we meet God in it, it becomes sacred. The laughter of a child, the smell of dinner cooking, the quiet moment in a chair after a long day, these can become altars of grace.

One woman began a simple spiritual practice: at the end of each day, she would ask herself, *"Where did I notice God today?"* Some days, the answer came quickly. Other days, it took effort. But over time, her heart began to wake up to the reality that God was not just in the past or future. He was with her in the now.

Scripture is filled with God showing up in the ordinary. Elijah heard God in the still, small voice. Jesus cooked breakfast for His disciples after the resurrection. God fed the Israelites with daily manna. His presence is not limited to grand moments. He is the God who shows up in the daily details.

## Letting Go of Hypervigilance

One of the most persistent wounds of trauma is hypervigilance, the chronic sense that something bad is about to happen. This heightened state of alertness once helped protect us, but over time, it becomes its own kind of captivity.

A trauma survivor may constantly scan crowds, brace for conflict, or avoid unfamiliar places. Some can't sleep unless certain routines are followed. Others feel panic when a door closes too loudly. These aren't signs of weakness; they're signs that the body has learned to survive. But God invites us into something more than survival.

Psalm 4:8 says, *"In peace I will both lie down and sleep; for you alone, O Lord, make me dwell in safety."* Letting go of hypervigilance doesn't mean ignoring our need for caution. It means recognizing that we don't have to carry it alone.

One man described a breakthrough moment: *"I finally gave myself permission to sit with my back to the door. It took months. But now I can do it, and sometimes I even forget to check the exits."*

Another survivor, a young mother, realized she had been checking her children's breathing every night for years. *"I used to think that if I let my guard down, something terrible would happen. But slowly, I've begun to believe that God is guarding them when I sleep."*

Jesus said, *"Do not be anxious about tomorrow, for tomorrow will be anxious for itself"* (Matthew 6:34). Releasing control is not passive; it is a deliberate act of trust in the One who never sleeps or slumbers.

## Practicing Faithfulness in the Now

Sometimes healing doesn't come in dramatic breakthroughs, but in small acts of faithfulness. Reclaiming the present often looks like obeying God in the next right thing.

For some, this may mean reading a single verse of Scripture each morning. For others, it might be showing up at church even when they feel numb. One survivor began each day by writing a note of encouragement to someone else, as a way of reminding herself she was still part of the body of Christ.

Another man committed to reading one Psalm each day and praying through it, not as a task, but as an act of presence. *"Some days it hits me. Some days it doesn't,"* he said. *"But it reminds me that God is speaking, and I'm still listening."*

Jesus taught us to pray, *"Give us this day our daily bread"* (Matthew 6:11). That prayer is an invitation to trust God one day at a time. It's not about having all the answers. It's about showing up in the present with an open heart and trusting that God is already there.

## Receiving the Gift of Today

Psalm 118:24 says, *"This is the day that the Lord has made; let us rejoice and be glad in it."* It doesn't say this is the perfect day. It says this is the day. The ordinary Tuesday. The hard Friday. The quiet Sunday morning. Each one is handcrafted by God, and each one holds the possibility of healing.

Lamentations 3:22-23 reminds us: *"The steadfast love of the Lord never ceases; his mercies never come to an end."* Like manna in the wilderness, His grace is given one day at a time, not for yesterday, not for tomorrow, but for today. Also, in 1 Kings 19, Elijah was exhausted and wanted to die. But God met him in the desert, not with rebuke, but with rest, food, and a whisper.

**That is the kindness of God. He meets us in the present, not where we think we should be, but exactly where we are.**

Gratitude in these moments is more than politeness, it's a form of worship. Noticing a flower, a kind word, or a breath of peace and saying, *"Thank You, Lord,"* is a declaration that the present is not empty. It is filled with God.

## Learning to Be Present with Others

Reclaiming the present is not only a personal journey, it is also relational. Trauma can isolate us, making us feel misunderstood, guarded, or emotionally distant from others. Many survivors carry a deep longing to connect but feel uncertain about how to re-engage. Being present with others is one of the most vulnerable and healing acts we can practice in recovery.

Jesus didn't just teach truth; He lived among people. He shared meals, walked dusty roads, attended weddings, and wept with friends. He showed us that spiritual healing is not just vertical, but horizontal. When we choose to be emotionally available to others, even in small ways, we create space for God's grace to flow through us and to us.

One survivor shared how she began setting aside her phone during family dinners. "*It was a small thing,*" she said, "*but it helped me feel like I was there, not just in the room. I was part of my family again.*" These intentional choices to engage, not perform, not impress, but simply be, are acts of courage.

The book of Romans reminds us, "*Rejoice with those who rejoice, weep with those who weep. Live in harmony with one another*" (Romans 12:15-16). Being present with others means we don't have to fix their pain or hide our own. We simply show up, heart open, willing to give and receive love.

Being with others also reminds us of our place in the body of Christ. When we are present with the church, whether in a sanctuary or a small group, we are reminded that we are not alone. We belong. Our presence matters, even when we feel fragile or invisible. And that belonging can help tether us to the present moment.

## The Enemy of Presence: Shame

One of the most significant obstacles to reclaiming the present is shame. Shame tells us that we are too broken to be seen, too damaged to be loved, or too far gone to matter. It pulls us backward into regret or forward into fear, making it nearly impossible to feel at peace in the now.

But the gospel confronts shame head-on. Jesus bore our shame on the cross, not just our sin. Hebrews 12:2 says, *"For the joy that was set before him endured the cross, despising the shame, and is seated at the right hand of the throne of God."* Christ didn't just take our guilt; He stripped shame of its power to define us.

When we feel ashamed, we often disconnect from the moment. We avoid eye contact. We retreat emotionally. We feel exposed. But God's love invites us to stand in the light. *"There is therefore now no condemnation for those who are in Christ Jesus"* (Romans 8:1). Living in that truth allows us to reclaim the present, not as a stage for perfection, but as a place for grace.

One man said that reclaiming the present began when he let go of self-punishment. *"I used to wake up and immediately rehearse everything I'd ever done wrong. But now I start my day with three words: 'Lord, I'm here.' That's enough."*

Being present is not about being perfect. It's about being honest. And God meets us in honesty every time.

## Presence as Worship

There is a sacredness to presence that is often overlooked. To be present is to resist despair, to rebel against the lie that we are defined by what happened to us, and to say with our lives, *"God is still with me."*

Presence can be a form of worship. When we slow down enough to notice God's goodness, when we acknowledge the beauty of His creation or the kindness of another human being, we are engaging in reverence. When we pause to breathe a prayer, offer thanks, or bless someone quietly in our hearts, we are turning the ordinary into an altar.

The Psalms are full of present-tense worship: *"This is the day"* (Psalm 118:24), *"Be still and know@* (Psalm 46:10), *"Taste and see"* (Psalm 34:8). These are invitations to experience God now, not only in doctrine, but in real-time relationship.

## Reflection

When trauma has held us captive, reclaiming the present is a radical act of defiance and faith. It is choosing to step out of the past and into the now, not because all is well, but because God is here. Each small act of obedience, each moment of awareness, each breath of gratitude is a sacred offering. With every choice to stay present, we declare: God is still writing my story. And He's not finished yet.

## Prayer

God of every moment, thank You for meeting me right where I am. Help me to release the grip of the past and the fear of the future. Teach me to dwell in Your presence, to notice the sacred in the everyday, and to receive today as the gift that it is. Calm my racing thoughts, soothe my anxious heart, and anchor me in the truth that I am safe in You.

Let me live this day fully, freely, and faithfully. Amen.

## Scripture

*"Peace I leave with you; my peace I give to you. Not as the world gives do I give to you. Let not your hearts be troubled, neither let them be afraid."* John 14:27

*"This is the day that the Lord has made; let us rejoice and be glad in it."* Psalm 118:24

*"The steadfast love of the Lord never ceases; his mercies never come to an end; they are new every morning; great is your faithfulness."* Lamentations 3:22-23

*"Therefore do not be anxious about tomorrow, for tomorrow will be anxious for itself. Sufficient for the day is its own trouble."* Matthew 6:34

## Reflection Questions

1.  In what ways do you notice yourself disconnected from the present?

_____

_____

_____

_____

2. How does trauma shape the way you think about time, past, present, or future?

_____

_____

_____

_____

_____

3. What specific thoughts or beliefs do you need to bring into alignment with Scripture?

_____

_____

_____

_____

_____

4. What act of obedience today could reconnect you to God's presence?

_____

_____

_____

_____

5. How might faithfulness in the small things become part of your healing?

_____

_____

_____

_____

_____

Chapter 20:
# LIVING WITHOUT FEAR

Fear is one of trauma's most powerful legacies. It lingers long after the event has passed, shaping how we perceive the world, how we interact with others, and our understanding of God. For many survivors, fear becomes the atmosphere in which we live. Even when we are safe, we feel threatened. Even when we are loved, we feel alone. Even when we believe in God, we struggle to trust Him.

Living without fear doesn't mean we never feel afraid. It means fear no longer rules us. It means that instead of being driven by anxiety, we are anchored in faith. It means we make our decisions from a place of peace, not panic. This kind of living is not the result of sheer willpower; it is the fruit of healing. And for the Christian, it is a promise rooted in the character of God Himself.

## Fear's Grip on the Heart

Fear is not just an emotion; it's a reaction embedded deep in the nervous system. After trauma, the brain becomes wired to anticipate danger.

This is part of the body's survival instinct, and it can be life-saving in the moment. However, over time, this heightened alertness can become a chronic condition. The heart races at harmless sounds. The stomach knots during normal conversations. The mind imagines worst-case scenarios in every situation.

Many survivors feel ashamed of their fear. They think it reflects a lack of faith. But Scripture never condemns fear as a feeling; it simply urges us not to let it become our master. Again and again, God's message to His people is, *"Do not be afraid."* These words are not a rebuke; they are a reassurance.

In Isaiah 41:10, God says, *"Fear not, for I am with you; be not dismayed, for I am your God; I will strengthen you, I will help you, I will uphold you with my righteous right hand."* God's answer to fear is not denial. It is presence.

## Naming the Fear

A critical step in healing is learning to name the fears we carry. Some are obvious: fear of death, danger, or rejection. Others are more hidden: fear of being a burden, fear of losing control, fear of feeling joy only to have it ripped away.

One woman described how she kept her life tightly ordered so nothing could surprise her. *"I wasn't just afraid of bad things happening, I was afraid of not being able to handle them. My fear was about my limits."*

Another man shared that after years of abuse, he feared success. *"Every time something good happened, I waited for it to be destroyed. I couldn't enjoy anything."*

When we name our fear, we take away part of its power. We bring it into the light, where God can meet it. Naming fear is not weakness; it is a step of courage. And it often opens the door to deeper healing.

## Jesus and Fear

Jesus was no stranger to fear. In the Garden of Gethsemane, His anguish ran so deep that His sweat fell like drops of blood. With a heart laid bare, He cried out to the Father, and still, He chose surrender: *"Not my will, but yours be done"* (Luke 22:42). All throughout the Gospels, Jesus speaks gently but firmly to fear, not only with words, but with action. He calms violent seas, restores broken bodies, drives out darkness, forgives the unforgivable, and ultimately, walks out of the grave. Every moment is a declaration: you don't have to be afraid.

In John 14:27, Jesus says, *"Peace I leave with you; my peace I give to you. Not as the world gives do I give to you. Let not your hearts be troubled, neither let them be afraid."* This peace is not circumstantial. It is not based on everything going right. It is rooted in who He is.

## Learning to Trust Again

One of the deepest wounds of trauma is a shattered sense of trust. Survivors often struggle to trust people, institutions, and even God. Fear whispers that trust will only lead to more pain. But healing involves learning to trust wisely and gradually again.

Trust doesn't mean blind vulnerability. It means choosing, little by little, to believe that goodness is still possible. That safety is not an illusion. That God is not distant. Psalm 56:3-4 says, *"When I am afraid, I put my trust in you. In God, whose word I praise, in God I trust; I shall not be afraid. What can flesh do to me?"* Trusting God doesn't always eliminate fear, but it reframes it. It reminds us that we are not alone in the dark.

One survivor shared that she began rebuilding trust by writing down every answered prayer, every kind gesture, and every safe person in her life. *"I needed evidence that God was still with me. And over time, that list got longer."*

## Courage as a Spiritual Practice

Courage is not the absence of fear; it is the decision to move forward in spite of it. In Scripture, courage is often paired with God's presence. *"Have I not commanded you? Be strong and courageous. Do not be frightened, and do not be dismayed, for the Lord your God is with you wherever you go."* (Joshua 1:9).

Courage in trauma recovery may look like going to therapy. Making a phone call. Setting a boundary. Telling the truth. Walking into a church. Praying again after silence. These small acts are deeply spiritual. They are declarations that fear will not have the final word. And each time we choose courage, our souls grow stronger.

## The Freedom of Love

One of the most powerful antidotes to fear is love. Scripture tells us, *"There is no fear in love, but perfect love casts out fear"* (1 John 4:18). This is not romantic love, but the unwavering, sacrificial, healing love of God. Fear shrinks us. It isolates, constricts, and paralyzes. Love expands. It draws us into relationship, into hope, into freedom.

Many trauma survivors fear being seen. Love says, *"I see you and I am still here."* Fear says, *"If people knew the truth, they'd leave."* Love says," *I already know, and I choose to stay"* God's love does not flinch at our scars. It does not withdraw in the face of our trembling. It moves toward us in our fear.

Living without fear doesn't mean we never encounter it, it means we are not governed by it. Love enables us to choose something more powerful than fear as our guide. Love leads us back to community, to purpose, to joy. And love leads us home to God.

For trauma survivors, the fear of what lies ahead can feel overwhelming. But Scripture reminds us that our story is not limited to the present moment or even this lifetime. Our lives are anchored in something eternal. When we remember what God has prepared for us, it changes how we face the struggles of today. Paul writes, *"So we do not lose heart. Though our outer self is wasting away, our inner self is being renewed day by day. For this light momentary affliction is preparing for us an eternal weight of glory beyond all comparison"* (2 Corinthians 4:16-17). This is not a call to minimize our suffering but to place it within a larger, hope-filled frame.

One woman who had experienced repeated loss described how this passage became her anchor: "*When the waves of fear came, I reminded myself, this isn't the end. God has more for me than what I can see. That helped me stand my ground.*" Peter also writes, "*According to His great mercy, He has caused us to be born again to a living hope through the resurrection of Jesus Christ from the dead*" (1 Peter 1:3). Living hope doesn't erase present fear, but it places it in context. We are moving toward restoration. We are held by eternity even as we walk through time.

## Walking in Daily Freedom

Living without fear is not just a mindset we achieve once, but a practice we return to every day. Each morning brings a fresh opportunity to choose faith over fear. The Christian life is not a one-time event but a daily walk with the Spirit who sets us free and strengthens us for what lies ahead.

Paul writes in Galatians 5:1, "*For freedom Christ has set us free; stand firm therefore, and do not submit again to a yoke of slavery.*" Fear can feel like a heavy chain dragging us backward, but Jesus has broken those chains. The challenge now is learning to walk in the freedom He has already given us. That freedom may look like speaking the truth when it's easier to stay silent. It may mean resting when fear demands we prove ourselves. It might be offering forgiveness when bitterness feels safer. Each choice becomes a way to live out our healing.

Romans 8:15 reminds us, "*For you did not receive the spirit of slavery to fall back into fear, but you have received the Spirit of adoption as sons, by whom we cry, 'Abba! Father!'*" We are no longer bound by fear. We are held by the One who calls us His own.

A man who had long struggled with anxiety shared that his turning point came when he began praying aloud each morning, *"God, I belong to You today."* That daily declaration helped him face challenges not with a clenched jaw, but with open hands. His fear didn't vanish overnight, but it lost its grip. Walking in freedom doesn't mean walking without difficulty. But it means knowing we are not walking alone. It means remembering that every step away from fear is a step deeper into grace.

## Reflection

Fear is real. But so is the power of God. In trauma recovery, living without fear is not a switch we flip; it is a journey we walk. Some days we walk strong. Other days we stumble. But every step is sacred when it is taken in faith. The presence of fear does not mean the absence of faith. Faith is what enables us to keep going. It is what enables us to say, *"God is with me, even here."* When we root our identity in the love of Christ, fear loses its power to define us. To live without fear is not to deny our past; it is to deny fear the right to tell us who we are. We are not victims. We are beloved. We are not abandoned. We are held. We are not hopeless. We are being healed.

## Prayer

God of peace and power, You know the fears that still linger in my heart. You see what others do not, the hidden places I still try to protect. Meet me there with Your perfect love. Cast out the fear that binds me. Give me the courage to trust You again, to take one more step, to believe that I am safe in You. Thank You for never turning away. Thank You for walking with me through every valley. Help me live from Your truth, not from my fear. In Jesus' name, Amen.

## Scripture

*"Fear not, for I am with you; be not dismayed, for I am your God; I will strengthen you, I will help you, I will uphold you with my righteous right hand."* Isaiah 41:10

*"Have I not commanded you? Be strong and courageous. Do not be frightened, and do not be dismayed, for the Lord your God is with you wherever you go."* Joshua 1:9

*"There is no fear in love, but perfect love casts out fear. For fear has to do with punishment, and whoever fears has not been perfected in love."* 1 John 4:18

## Reflection Questions

1.  What specific fears still have influence over your thoughts or actions?

_____

_____

_____

_____

_____

2. How has trauma shaped your ability to trust yourself, others, or God?

_____

_____

_____

_____

_____

3. What does courage look like in your life right now?

_____

_____

_____

_____

_____

4. In what ways have you seen God's love disarm fear in your journey?

_____

_____

_____

_____

_____

5. Which Scripture from this chapter speaks most deeply to your heart?

_____

_____

_____

_____

_____

Chapter 21:
# BEAUTY FROM ASHES

S cars are sacred. Not because of the pain it represents, but because of what it proves: we survived. We endured. We emerged. For the person who has experienced trauma, the scar becomes a kind of monument. It marks the place of wounding, yes, but also of healing. It testifies not only to what was lost, but to what remains. It testifies not only to what was lost, but to what remains: the God who brings beauty from ashes and writes redemption into the brokenness of our stories.

Every scar can become a testimony. Not because the pain disappears, but because God begins to rewrite the meaning of the wound. A scar tells a story—not just of the injury, but of the healing. When we choose to speak honestly about what we've been through, when we name the pain without shame and trace the ways God has carried us through it, our story becomes a light for someone else still walking in darkness. Testimony does not require having all the answers; it simply means saying, *"This is where I was . . . and this is how God met me there."*

And every war-torn space in our soul can become sacred ground if we let God meet us there. But how do we do that? It starts with honesty. We stop pretending we're okay. We stop hiding the places that still hurt. We bring our questions, our grief, our anger, and our confusion, all of it, into God's presence. Not cleaned up, but raw and real. This may take the form of a whispered prayer through tears. It may look like sitting in silence, simply asking God to draw near. Or it may mean inviting a trusted friend, counselor, or pastor into our pain, letting them help carry what feels too heavy to bear alone.

The smell of smoke lingers long after the flames die out. It clings to clothing, hair, and memory. Trauma is like that, its residue persists even when the crisis has passed. Survivors often find that the emotional and spiritual aftermath lasts much longer than the event itself. Long after others move on, we're still carrying the scent of survival. Letting God meet us in our woundedness is not about forcing a quick resolution. It's about creating space, spiritually, emotionally, and relationally—for healing to begin. And over time, as we allow God to sit with us in the ashes, we may find that healing does not mean forgetting the pain. It means discovering that God was there all along, and that even this broken ground can grow something beautiful.

And know this: God does not observe our suffering from a distance. He weeps with us in our pain, not out of pity, but out of deep love. Just as a parent aches for a child who is hurting, God aches for us. He is not indifferent to your tears—He treasures them. Scripture tells us that Jesus wept (John 11:35, even knowing He would raise Lazarus from the dead, He still entered fully into the grief of those He loved. That is the heart of our Savior. He meets us not only with promises of restoration but with the comfort of His presence in the middle of the sorrow. When we are undone, God does not turn away. He draws near, holds us close, and joins us in the weeping.

That's why Isaiah 61 matters. The prophet speaks of the coming Messiah who would "*give them a beautiful headdress instead of ashes, the oil of gladness instead of mourning, the garment of praise instead of a faint spirit*"!(v. 3). This is not merely poetic comfort; it is a radical promise of transformation. God doesn't just sweep the ashes away; He brings beauty from them. He doesn't silence mourning; He transforms it into praise.

The ancient Japanese art of Kintsugi illustrates this kind of beauty. Kintsugi means "golden joinery." It is the craft of repairing broken pottery with lacquer mixed with powdered gold. Instead of hiding the break, Kintsugi highlights it. The cracks become the most stunning part of the vessel, not a sign of damage, but of redemption. It doesn't just fix the vessel, it redefines its value.

When we experience deep wounds, trauma, grief, and betrayal, it can feel like our lives have shattered into pieces. We think healing means going back to what we were. But God's healing is not about reassembling the old. It's about resurrection. It's about creating something new, even more meaningful than before.

In Kintsugi, the artisan takes time. Every fragment is cleaned and honored. The gold is laid in layer by layer, until the object becomes whole again, not hidden, not ashamed, but radiant. That's what the Holy Spirit does in us. Slowly. Patiently. Redemptively.

Just like shattered pottery, we often resist the restoration process. Quick fixes feel more appealing. Longing for our old selves, we try to pretend the pain never touched us. But healing does not come through forgetting. Restoration is not about erasure—it's about learning to remember through the lens of grace, not shame or fear. That's what makes beauty from ashes so powerful. The ashes remain, but they are no longer signs of ruin. They become soil for new growth, evidence of grace at work.

**One of the most powerful lessons I have learned through years of trauma care and chaplaincy is this: our scars can become sacred. Not because the suffering was good, but because God's presence in the midst of it was.**

We meet God most intimately in our places of brokenness. And those encounters can change us forever.

Rachel was a woman whose trauma had silenced her for decades. As a child, she endured repeated abuse from someone who should have protected her. For years, she lived behind a mask, polite, high-achieving, outwardly faithful. But inside, she was numb. Every compliment felt like a lie. Every achievement felt like survival. Deep down, she was convinced she was irreparably broken.

When she began counseling, her responses were cautious and controlled. She had learned to speak "church language," masking her pain behind Scripture and smiles. But slowly, through consistent support and a safe, grace-filled environment, she began to speak truthfully. Her anger surfaced. So did her sorrow. For the first time, she grieved what was taken from her. She cried out to God not in polished prayers, but in raw honesty. And He met her there.

There was no instant healing moment, no dramatic transformation overnight. But there was slow, steady grace. Through group therapy, journaling, worship, and quiet solitude with God, Rachel began to discover that her value had never been lost. Her voice had never been erased. She started writing poetry, something she had not done since high school. She began mentoring younger women. She gave her testimony in a trauma recovery workshop. And she stopped apologizing for being someone who had survived something terrible.

Rachel once told me, "*I thought my pain made me worthless. But it turns out that is the very place where God met me, and the very place He now uses to meet others.*" She became a picture of Kintsugi, her scars no longer hidden, but gilded with grace. Her life bore witness to the truth that healing is not about perfection; it's about redemption.

A former Marine, Mike came home from war but never really returned. What he'd seen overseas, what he'd lost, haunted him. He walked with a limp from a roadside bomb, but the deeper wounds were invisible. For years, he refused help, burying himself in work, alcohol, and silence. His faith, once vibrant, had faded into guilt and anger. "*If God is real,*" he told me during our first session, "*He sure wasn't there when my squad got hit.*" But he kept coming, not out of hope, but out of desperation. Something in him knew that the silence was killing him.

At a veterans' retreat in the mountains, we read Isaiah 61 around the campfire. When they reached the part about "*binding up the brokenhearted*" and *"proclaiming liberty to the captives,"* Mike looked away. But he didn't walk off. After a long silence, he said, *"I don't know if I believe that verse. But I want to."*

That night, something began to break, not in anger, but in vulnerability. He began talking. Not about tactics or timelines, but about the faces of those he couldn't save. About the guilt that gripped him like a vice. About the emptiness that lingered, even when everyone else said he should be grateful to be home.

They didn't give Mike trite answers. They gave him space. They stayed present. In that atmosphere of safety and grace, something in him began to shift. Over time, he started showing up for himself, joining a trauma recovery group, speaking truths he never thought he would voice aloud. And when a younger vet arrived, trembling and unsure, Mike didn't try to fix it. He simply met his eyes and said, *"You're not alone."* And in that moment, it was enough.

His healing didn't erase his past. It reframed it. Mike's story became a quiet testimony, not a polished sermon, but a lived-out parable of grace. The man who once cursed God in a desert now serves as a mentor for wounded warriors, showing others that scars don't disqualify them. They connect them.

What both Rachel and Mike show us is this: scars don't have to be hidden. In fact, they can be holy.

Jesus didn't hide His scars. After His resurrection, when He appeared to the disciples, He could have come back in glory, with no trace of the suffering He endured. But He didn't. He showed them His hands. He said to Thomas, *"Put your finger here, and see my hands; and put out your hand, and place it in my side"* (John 20:27). Jesus kept His wounds, not because they hadn't healed, but because they had. And they were now part of His glory.

Our healing stories aren't whole without the scars; they speak to what we endured. More than reminders of pain, they become evidence of survival. They show that the fire didn't consume us. And for those still walking through the flames, they offer hope: healing is possible, and light can return.

This is what makes Kintsugi so theologically rich. It affirms that our brokenness is not the end of our story. It confirms that restoration is not about returning to what was; it's about becoming something more beautiful, more honest, and more real.

But this kind of beauty comes at a cost. It requires surrender. It requires that we stop pretending, stop performing, and let God into the places we have kept sealed off. It means confessing our pain, admitting our weariness, and allowing others to witness our healing, not just our strength.

And that's terrifying. Because we live in a culture that celebrates success, not struggle. We're told to *"move on," "stay strong," and "look on the bright side."* But biblical healing looks different. It allows for lament. It honors the grieving process. It doesn't rush. And it never shames. Isaiah 61 promises joy, but not without mourning. It promises gladness, but not by skipping over sorrow. The beauty God brings is born from ashes. It rises from what has been reduced, refined, and redeemed.

When we allow God to meet us in our pain, He begins a work that is far more than repair. He begins to recreate. He doesn't just patch over the damage, He makes something sacred out of it. You might not feel like you're there yet. Maybe you're still in the ashes, still in the breaking, still waiting for the gold to show up. That's okay.

Healing rarely moves in predictable steps. Some days, the pain feels fresh again. Some memories still catch you off guard. That doesn't mean we've failed. It means we are still healing. The gold is coming. The beauty is forming. And even now, before it's complete, we are deeply loved.

In pastoral care, I've often seen people try to return to who they were before the trauma. *"I just want to be the old me again,"* they say. But God rarely takes us back. Instead, He takes us forward, into something new. Something deeper. Something more like Christ. That's the kind of transformation Isaiah envisioned. The broken become oaks of righteousness. The mourners become planters of praise. The wounded become witnesses. When we allow God to meet us in our pain, He begins a work that is far more than repair. He begins to recreate. He doesn't just patch over the damage, He makes something sacred out of it.

You might not feel like you're there yet. Maybe you're still in the ashes, still in the breaking, still waiting for the gold to show up. That's okay. As I've said before, healing is not linear. Some days, the pain feels fresh again. Some memories still catch you off guard. That doesn't mean we've failed. It means we are still healing. The gold is coming. The beauty is forming. And even now, before it's complete, we are deeply loved.

One of the most profound truths of Christian healing is that it unfolds both in God's presence and through the presence of others. While He meets us in silence and solitude, He also ministers through community— in a held story, a listening ear, or the quiet companionship of someone who whispers, *"You don't have to carry this alone."*

That's what Mike offered the younger veteran. That's what Rachel stepped into as she began mentoring other women. Neither came with perfect answers, but both came with presence. With scars that spoke of survival. With hope that had been hard-won. It calls to mind Paul's words in 2 Corinthians 1:3–4: *"Blessed be the God and Father of our Lord Jesus Christ, the Father of mercies and God of all comfort, who comforts us in all our affliction, so that we may be able to comfort those who are in any affliction."*

That is the heart of redemptive ministry—healed people offering healing presence.

When your scar becomes a source of strength for someone else, it's not exploitation. Its incarnation. You are carrying the presence of Christ into the wounds of others. You become a testimony that healing is possible, not perfect, not painless, but real.

That is why I believe so profoundly in trauma-informed ministry. Not because it's trendy, but because it reflects the heart of Jesus. He saw the ones others passed by. He touched the unclean. He let a bleeding woman reach out to Him. He sat with the shamed and called them by name. He never demanded that they "move on." He met them in their pain and gave them back their dignity.

That's what this chapter is about. Not just the idea that God can bring beauty from ashes, but the lived reality that He does, repeatedly. In Rachel. In Mike. In you. In me. When we stop hiding our pain and start letting God use it, something shifts in us. We are no longer defined by what happened to us; we are defined by what Christ has done in us. And as you walk forward, not rushed, not forced, but in faith, you begin to reflect the beauty of His redemption, not just in your private healing, but in your public presence. You become a carrier of hope.

**Your trauma may have marked you, but it does not name you. God gives you a new name. Beloved. Restored. Redeemed.**

I've seen former addicts serve as ministers. I've watched trauma survivors lead worship. I've seen men and women who once sat silent in pews now speak with authority and grace. This is the miracle of restoration. Not that we become "perfect," but that we become useful. Honest. Compassionate. Healed enough to serve. This is what Isaiah 61 means by *"oaks of righteousness."* Oaks don't grow overnight. They grow through storms and seasons. But when they mature, they become strong enough to offer shelter for others. That's what healing does: it turns us into people of refuge. Our presence says, *"There's space for you here. I've walked this road. You're not alone."*

If you are still in the early stages of your journey, don't lose heart. God is not done. There is gold in your story that has not yet been revealed. And if you are further along, ask God to show you who needs to hear what He has done for you. Not because you're an expert, but because you're a witness. Your scar may be the survival map someone else has been praying for.

## Reflection

God never wastes our wounds. What was once your place of breaking can become your place of blessing. Like Kintsugi, our story becomes more valuable, not despite the cracks, but because of how they have been healed. You were never meant to stay shattered. You were meant to shine.

## Prayer

Father, You are the God who binds up the brokenhearted and brings beauty from ashes. Thank You for not discarding my wounds, but redeeming them. Teach me to stop hiding my scars and instead let them speak of Your healing power. May my life reflect Your grace, broken, restored, and radiant with the gold of Your mercy. Amen.

## Scripture

*"To grant to those who mourn in Zion, to give them a beautiful headdress instead of ashes, the oil of gladness instead of mourning, the garment of praise instead of a faint spirit; that they may be called oaks of righteousness, the planting of the Lord, that he may be glorified."* Isaiah 61:3

## Reflection Questions

1. What part of your story still feels like ashes?

---

---

---

2. How have you seen God begin to bring beauty from your pain?

_____

_____

_____

_____

_____

3. In what ways do your scars reflect the faithfulness of God?

_____

_____

_____

_____

_____

4. How might God use your healing to help someone else?

_____

_____

_____

_____

_____

5.  What would it look like to live today as a testimony?

_____

_____

_____

_____

_____

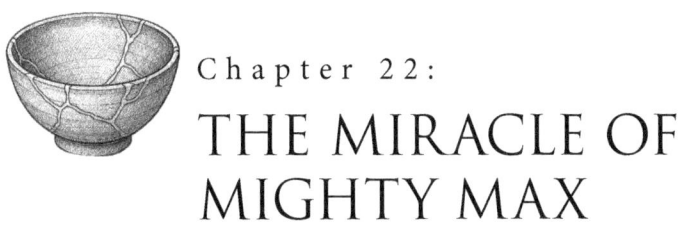

Chapter 22:

# THE MIRACLE OF MIGHTY MAX

N
ot every form of healing looks like a counseling room, a support group, or even a church altar. Sometimes it arrives on four legs with a leash and a wagging tail. For those living with the invisible wounds of trauma, animals have become powerful partners in the journey toward peace. They don't quote Scripture or offer therapy techniques, but they sit close, steady our breathing, and remind us, moment by moment, that we're not alone.

For me, healing came with fur, paws, and the kind of gentleness only God could have orchestrated. His name is Max.

## A Miracle in Motion

I was told, as many veterans are, that getting a service animal would take years, four to five, on average. These animals are trained extensively, often at a cost of tens of thousands of dollars. Many nonprofits help veterans like me obtain them free of charge, but the waitlists are long, and the need is overwhelming.

Still, after years of wrestling with PTSD and living with a level of anxiety that never seemed to let up, I finally decided to try. I added my name to a few lists, not expecting much. I was in my late sixties, still active in ministry, frequently traveling for work, and often in airports, hotels, and restaurants, hardly a lifestyle suited for a 75-pound service dog.

But God had other plans. Three months later, yes, just three, I received a call from a training facility in North Carolina. They asked, *"Are you still looking for a service dog?"* I almost laughed. Of course I was, though I wasn't expecting that question for another four years. They knew my story and believed they had the right dog for me. I asked how long the process would take. Their response: *"If you can come tomorrow, you can have him."*

It turns out Max had been an emotional support animal for a pair of children. Their family had been forced to give him up because their landlord discovered that he wasn't a service dog, and under the law, only service animals are guaranteed housing protections. They were given two weeks to either get rid of the dog or move. Unable to move, they surrendered Max to the training organization. That's when my name came up. They saw in Max the perfect match for my needs, and the rest, I believe, was orchestrated by God's loving hand.

Max and I began working together right away. We still needed a few months of additional training, but he was already intuitive, sensitive, and deeply attuned to my emotional needs. What followed was one of the greatest gifts God has ever given me.

## Redirecting the Mind

One of the most remarkable ways God uses Max in my life is through redirected focus. PTSD often makes us hyper-aware of our internal state, our thoughts, our fears, and our pain. But Max has a way of interrupting that. When I'm emotionally overwhelmed, anxious, or beginning to escalate, he knows before I do.

If I'm sitting in a chair and my heart starts racing or my thoughts spiral, Max comes over and puts his paws on my chest or sometimes throws his entire body across my lap so his front legs drape over one side and his back legs over the other. If that's not possible, he noses his way between my arm and my side, anchoring me in the present. His presence demands attention in the best way: it forces my mind off the internal storm and onto something safe, grounded, and real.

When I'm standing and talking with someone, and anxiety starts to rise, Max performs one of his trained behaviors. He circles behind me, goes between my legs, sits down, and looks up at me with his head pressed against my chest. At that moment, I have no choice but to notice him. I have to respond. And when I do, something in me resets. It's truly amazing what these animals, with proper training and divine timing, are capable of doing. Sometimes I don't even realize my stress is rising until Max is already in position. He sees it first. That's what makes him a service dog, not just his training, but his intuition and connection with me.

I'm not cured. I probably won't be this side of Heaven. But Max has changed my daily life. And that is a miracle.

# Understanding the Difference: Emotional Support Animals, Therapy Animals, Service Animals

For those considering how animals might aid in healing from trauma or PTSD, it's important to understand the three most common categories of support animals:

## 1. Emotional Support Animals

Purpose: Provide comfort through companionship; not trained for specific tasks

Training: No formal task-based training required

Legal Protection: Covered under the Fair Housing Act (FHA); not protected in public spaces

Role: Eases general emotional distress (anxiety, depression, PTSD)

## 2. Therapy Animals

Purpose: Used in hospitals, schools, or group therapy to provide emotional comfort to others

Training: Trained for temperament and public behavior

Legal Protection: No legal rights for access in public spaces or housing

Role: Not assigned to one person; supports emotional care in structured settings

## 3. Service Animals

Purpose: Trained to perform specific tasks for someone with a disability

Training: Extensive, individualized training required

Legal Protection: Fully protected under ADA, FHA, and ACAA

Role: Directly supports a person's disability by performing critical tasks (e.g., grounding during panic attacks, waking from nightmares, retrieving medication)

Max is legally recognized as a service animal, trained specifically for PTSD intervention. That's why he can accompany me into restaurants, on planes, and in hotel rooms, and he does so with quiet dignity. Most people never even know he's there.

## Technology as a Grounding Tool: The Promise of HRV Monitoring

While animals like Max offer grounding through presence and companionship, another surprising tool for managing trauma-related anxiety comes not on four legs, but in the palm of your hand.

In recent years, smartphone and smartwatch technology has quietly become a lifeline for many living with PTSD, thanks in part to something called heart rate variability (HRV). HRV is a measurement of the variation in time between heartbeats, and it serves as a powerful indicator of how well the autonomic nervous system is functioning. A healthy HRV suggests that your body is adapting well to stress. A drop in HRV, on the other hand, often means that stress is rising, even if you're not consciously aware of it.

My phone now provides me with feedback throughout the day on how I'm doing, whether I'm calm, balanced, or edging into a stressed state. Many smartwatches now offer real-time stress detection based on HRV patterns, alerting the wearer with a gentle vibration or a prompt to breathe, stretch, or take a step back. These aren't miracle cures, and they certainly aren't foolproof, but they are remarkably helpful for increasing self-awareness.

For those of us who've lived with chronic anxiety or hypervigilance, HRV tracking can offer a kind of mirror: a way to see what's happening inside, when our minds are too preoccupied to notice. It becomes a moment of intervention. An opportunity to pause. Sometimes, just knowing your body is in distress, even when your mind isn't yet aware, can give you the window you need to reset. This is not a replacement for deeper healing, but it's a tool. And tools matter.

## More Ways People Are Finding Peace

God has embedded this world with all kinds of restorative gifts, many of which are easy to overlook because they seem too ordinary, too **Not every healing tool needs to be clinical or spiritual in the traditional sense.** gentle, or too different from what we've been taught to expect. But for trauma survivors, these small, sacred interventions often become lifelines.

Here are a few lesser-known ways people are finding peace, grounding, and emotional relief on their trauma journeys:

## Nature Immersion (Forest Bathing / Shinrin-Yoku)

Spending unhurried time in a quiet forest or garden, simply breathing, noticing, and being, can quiet the mind and lower cortisol levels. Known in Japan as shinrin-yoku, or "forest bathing," it's less about exercise and more about presence. Scripture itself is full of encounters with God in natural places, from Moses at the burning bush to Jesus retreating to the hills to pray.

## Creative Expression

Art, music, and movement offer pathways to healing when words fail. Whether through journaling, painting, playing an instrument, or gentle, expressive dance, these embodied practices allow emotions to flow safely. Creativity gives trauma a container, and beauty, even if fragile, begins to rise from the ashes.

## Weighted Blankets and Deep Pressure Touch

Simple but effective, weighted blankets or compression vests can calm an overstimulated nervous system. Many trauma survivors find that deep pressure offers a sense of safety and containment, especially at night.

## Cold Water Exposure

Immersing the face or body briefly in cold water, or even taking a cold shower, can help regulate emotional overwhelm by activating the vagus nerve. It creates a sharp reset that brings focus and presence when panic feels out of control.

## Tactile Grounding Tools

Small objects, textured stones, scented oils, wooden crosses, or beaded bracelets, can serve as physical anchors during moments of distress. They help interrupt spiraling thoughts and reconnect us with the body and present moment.

## Gardening and Plant Care

Working with soil, watering plants, and watching life grow offers not just calm, but metaphor: healing takes time, attention, and sunlight. Gardening becomes a therapeutic rhythm that reflects the spiritual seasons of pruning and renewal.

## Laughter and Therapeutic Joy

Laughter isn't just medicine, it's a sacred release. Whether through movies, time with children, or moments of playful joy, many survivors cultivate laughter as a way to shake off heaviness. It reminds us that we were made for joy, too.

## Reflection

Healing does not always come in the ways we expect. Sometimes, it looks like a golden retriever curling up on your chest when your heart is racing. Other times, it hums quietly through your smartwatch's alert or whispers from a forest trail. These tools may not quote Scripture, but they echo the compassion of a God who meets us exactly where we are. Max isn't just a dog—he's a vessel of God's kindness, an ever-present reminder that we are seen, known, and worthy of care.

As trauma survivors, we often learn to live in survival mode, disconnected from our bodies and too exhausted to even recognize when stress is climbing. But God, in His mercy, provides more than just theological truth—He gives us tangible help. Whether it's through the soft weight of a blanket, the smell of a lavender balm, or the silent companionship of a creature who simply stays—these ordinary gifts reveal an extraordinary truth: healing is holy, even when it looks unconventional.

We serve a creative God who uses unexpected means to draw us toward wholeness. Scripture shows us that Jesus didn't always heal with words. Sometimes He used spit and mud, sometimes a touch, sometimes just His presence. And sometimes, He met people not in the temple, but out in the fields or on the road. That same Savior walks with us today—through Max's eyes, through forest light, through laughter. All of it is grace.

## Prayer

Lord,

Thank You for knowing the depths of our pain and the tenderness of our needs. You are not a distant God. You are Immanuel—God with us—in the quiet, in the panic, in the places we didn't expect to find You. Thank You for Max. Thank You for every tool, every touch, every breath that helps bring us back when trauma pulls us under. Forgive us when we overlook Your healing because it comes in unfamiliar forms. Remind us that You are the Author of all comfort, and You delight in using whatever means will lead us closer to peace.

Teach us to pay attention—to the signs in our bodies, the nudges of Your Spirit, the gentle guidance of creation. Give us courage to embrace the tools You offer, no matter how unconventional they may seem. Let our healing be a testament to Your creativity and compassion. And may we never forget that even in our woundedness, we are loved, carried, and never alone.

Amen.

## Scripture

*"Even the sparrow finds a home, and the swallow a nest for herself, where she may lay her young, at your altars, O Lord of hosts, my King and my God."*

—Psalm 84:3 (ESV)

*"For God gave us a spirit not of fear but of power and love and self-control."*

—2 Timothy 1:7 (ESV)

*"The Lord is near to the brokenhearted and saves the crushed in spirit."*

—Psalm 34:18 (ESV)

## Reflection Questions

1. Have you ever experienced healing or comfort through something unconventional, like an animal, nature, or art? What was that like?

_____

_____

_____

_____

_____

2. In what ways might God be inviting you to pay attention to your body's signals and to respond with compassion instead of critique?

_____

_____

_____

_____

_____

3. Which of the grounding tools mentioned in this chapter speaks most to your current needs? How could you integrate it into your daily life?

_____

_____

_____

_____

_____

4. What has Max's story stirred in your heart about the nature of God's provision and timing?

_____

_____

_____

_____

5. Do you struggle to believe that tools like service animals or HRV monitoring can be "spiritual"? Why or why not?

_____

_____

_____

6. How might you expand your view of what healing can look like—both for yourself and for those you walk alongside?

_____

# THE MIRACLE OF MIGHTY MAX

Chapter 23:

# SCARS THAT SHINE

There's something sacred about a scar. Not because of the pain it represents, but because of what it proves: you survived. You endured. You emerged. For the person who has experienced trauma, the scar becomes a kind of monument. It marks the place of wounding, yes, but also of healing. It testifies not only to what was lost but to what remains to the God who brings beauty from ashes and writes redemption into the brokenness of our stories.

This is the final chapter of this book, but it is not the end of your journey, far from it. In many ways, this is just the beginning, the beginning of walking in the world with your scars uncovered, not in shame but in sacred honesty. There is a quiet strength that grows from the rubble of trauma. It's not the strength of denial or repression. It's the strength of love refined by fire, of faith that's endured the long night and still lifts its face toward the dawn.

## Scars That Speak

Throughout this book, we have often reflected on Kintsugi. And now, as we come to the end, we see how it all comes together. Your life is that vessel. Your wounds have not been ignored or hidden; they've been lovingly restored with something even more valuable. The seams of gold that trace your past are not weaknesses, but beauty born of suffering. They show where healing has taken hold. They reflect grace.

This chapter is for anyone who still wonders if their story is worth anything. For anyone who feels disqualified because of what they've endured. Hear this truth: God does not discard the broken. He dwells with them. He calls them blessed. *"He heals the brokenhearted and binds up their wounds"* (Psalm 147:3). He uses their wounds to bear witness to the power of His love. Think of Thomas in the upper room. Jesus didn't hide His scars. He showed them. And it was in seeing those scars that Thomas came to believe. Your scars can be that powerful, too.

## A Light in the Darkness

To those who suffer: your pain is not wasted. Your healing is not invisible. Even the slowest steps forward are signs of courage. Your faith, even if it feels like the faintest ember, is still faith, and it is seen by God. *"The light shines in the darkness, and the darkness has not overcome it"* (John 1:5). Trauma does not get the final word. Christ does. And His word over you is life, grace, and restoration. You are not alone. You are not broken beyond repair. You are not a burden. You are beloved.

The enemy often whispers that healing must be quick or dramatic to count—but that's not how Jesus moves. His pace is patient. With tenderness, He draws near to the hurting, lingers beside the grieving, and breathes life into places we believed were beyond repair. *"A bruised reed he will not break, and a faintly burning wick he will not quench"* (Isaiah 42:3). The road may stretch long, but you never walk it alone. The Savior is beside you, steady and sure, every step of the way.

## A Story of Scars That Serve

Erica had worked as a trauma nurse for more than a decade. She didn't wear a uniform like a soldier or carry a badge like a police officer, but she was no stranger to blood and chaos. Over the years, she had held the hands of accident victims gasping their last breaths, stabilized children injured in violent homes, and comforted the family of a man who didn't survive emergency surgery. People often said, *"I don't know how you do it."* But the truth was, she didn't know either.

At first, the adrenaline had fueled her, and the mission sustained her. But over time, a quiet heaviness took hold. She stopped sleeping through the night. Certain smells triggered nausea. Flashbacks interrupted her prayers. Even her faith, once vibrant and sturdy, felt dim under the weight of so many stories she couldn't forget.

One day, a chaplain noticed her sitting outside on a break, staring at the pavement with tears she didn't even know had started falling. *"Sometimes the ones who serve suffer in silence,"* he said gently. *"You carry the pain of so many. Who's helping you carry yours?"*

That moment changed everything. Erica entered counseling, began to name her pain, and even allowed others into her wounds. She realized she had been absorbing second-hand trauma, vicarious trauma, not because she was weak, but because she loved deeply. And now, healed and healing, she speaks with compassion to every young nurse who wonders if they're allowed to hurt, too. "Jesus *wept," she told them. "And He weeps with us. But He also heals."*

Her story is a reminder: scars can speak, even when they are not our own. And those who carry the wounds of others are not forgotten by the God who sees in secret.

## For Those Who Walk Alongside

This chapter is also for those who love someone with a history of trauma. Your presence matters more than you know. Don't underestimate the ministry of simply staying close. When you offer safety, when you listen without trying to fix, when you reflect Christ's love without conditions, you become a vessel of healing.

You don't have to say the perfect thing. You don't have to carry the full weight of their grief. What you "can" do is be there. Remind them that they are not alone. Walk with them at their own pace. Celebrate even the smallest moments of growth. Speak life. Pray faithfully. And when they cannot hope for themselves, hope "for" them.

Never forget: healing happens in a relationship. We are not meant to recover in isolation. The body of Christ was made for this: to bear one another's burdens, to comfort as we have been comforted, and to shine light into the darkest valleys. *"Bear one another's burdens, and so fulfill the law of Christ"* (Galatians 6:2). Your love can be the evidence that someone needs to believe that redemption is possible.

## Redeemed and Radiant

In Scripture, God's redemption is never halfway. He doesn't offer a temporary fix or a superficial covering. Instead, He reclaims what's been broken and infuses it with purpose. What was meant to destroy becomes a source of life. His glory is placed in vessels once fractured, and through those very cracks, His light breaks through.

**"Redeemed" doesn't just mean rescued; it means restored with worth.**

This is where the image of Kintsugi finds its truest expression. The golden seams of healing aren't covered—they're celebrated. Rather than diminishing the testimony, they complete it. Paul writes, *"We have this treasure in jars of clay, to show that the surpassing power belongs to God and not to us"* (2 Corinthians 4:7). Fragility isn't a flaw to be hidden. It becomes the very place where God's power is most visible.

Even Jesus' post-resurrection body bore the marks of suffering. The glorified Christ did not erase His scars. He displayed them. And in doing so, He dignified every scar you carry. Each mark on your soul, each story that once brought shame, now carries the potential to bring healing to someone else. Your scars can shine, not because they're beautiful on their own, but because they reflect the One who redeemed them.

Take, for example, Miguel, a retired firefighter. For three decades, he responded to calls most people run from, burning buildings, collapsed structures, and mangled highways. He'd rescued children from homes engulfed in smoke and pulled bodies from wreckage. He'd seen more grief than he ever thought his heart could hold. Yet what haunted him most wasn't what he couldn't do; it was the moment he believed he had failed. It was a house fire on Christmas Eve. A mother and her son were trapped upstairs. Miguel tried to reach them, but the staircase collapsed. When he found out later they hadn't survived, something broke inside him. He finished the shift, but he was never the same.

For years, Miguel didn't talk about it. But the nightmares came anyway. So did the guilt. So did the feeling that maybe God had turned His back, or worse, that Miguel had let God down. Healing began slowly, in the honest prayers he began whispering in his truck, and later, through a men's group where he finally said the words out loud: *"I couldn't save them."* And one older man replied, *"You're not the Savior. But you bear His heart."*

Today, Miguel speaks openly at first responder conferences. He tells others that their pain matters. That their brokenness isn't weakness, it's a sign they haven't gone numb. He reminds them that the hands of Christ are still wounded, still open, still reaching for us in our darkest hour.

You may still carry pain. You may still be waiting for some wounds to fully close. But even now, you carry the light of Christ within you. Your story is a testimony. Not of perfection, but of perseverance. Not of easy answers, but of deep faith. And that is a story the world desperately needs.

If your scars could speak, what would they say? Perhaps they would whisper of nights you thought you wouldn't make it. Of days when joy seemed a million miles away. Of losses too deep for words. And yet, they would also speak of the God who sustained you. The people who stood by you. The strength you found when you thought you had none.

Your scars shine not because they are flawless, but because they are filled with meaning. They reflect the One who was wounded for you, who carries scars of His own, and who now calls you His own. *"But he said to me, 'My grace is sufficient for you, for my power is made perfect in weakness.' Therefore, I will boast all the more gladly of my weaknesses, so that the power of Christ may rest upon me"* (2 Corinthians 12:9). You are a living testimony that trauma does not define the end of the story. Redemption does.

You may still carry pain. You may still be waiting for some wounds to fully close. But even now, you carry the light of Christ within you. Your story is a testimony. Not of perfection, but of perseverance. Not of easy answers, but of deep faith. And that is a story the world desperately needs.

If your scars could speak, what would they say? Perhaps they would whisper of nights you thought you wouldn't make it. Of days when joy seemed a million miles away. Of losses too deep for words. And yet, they would also speak of the God who sustained you. The people who stood by you. The strength you found when you thought you had none.

## Commissioned by Grace

As this chapter closes, let it also open a door: a sending, a commissioning, a gentle but holy push toward the life that still awaits. You are not being sent alone. You are being sent with Christ, the One who walks through locked doors to show His scars and say, *"Peace be with you."*

You may not feel ready. That's okay. Very few ever do. But every scar you carry, every lesson learned in the fire, every tear God has collected, these are now part of your ministry. Healing is never just for us. It spills over. It blesses others. It speaks life into someone else's despair.

So walk boldly, scarred and shining. Let people see that Jesus is still alive, alive in the honest stories, in the steady compassion, in the surprising joy of someone who once believed they'd never feel whole again. Let your life tell the truth: that scars are not the end of the story. They are the place where the next chapter begins.

## Reflection

You have journeyed through the valley. You have faced pain with courage and looked honestly at what trauma has done. But now, with hope, you can also look at what God is building in its place. Your story is not only one of survival, but also one of significance. As you continue to heal, may your scars become signs that healing is possible, that God is faithful, and that beauty still blooms in broken places.

## Prayer

Father, thank You for being with me through every part of this journey. Thank You for healing what I thought would never heal, and for loving me when I couldn't love myself. Help me to walk forward in faith, not hiding my scars, but letting them shine with Your glory. Give me courage to hope again, and grace to walk alongside others in their pain. May my life reflect the beauty of Your redemption. In Jesus' name, Amen.

## Reflection Questions

1. What are some of the "scars" in your life that God is beginning to use for good?

 

 

 

 

2. How does the journey of Kintsugi throughout this book reflect your own healing story?

 

 

 

 

3. In what ways have you seen God's presence even in your darkest moments?

_____

_____

_____

_____

_____

4. Who has walked with you in your trauma, and how have they shown the love of Christ?

_____

_____

_____

_____

5. How can your story become a light of hope for someone else who is suffering?

_____

_____

_____

_____

YOU are not the same person who began this book. YOU are braver. Wiser. More whole. And YOUR scars? They shine.

# A CLOSING LETTER
# FROM THE AUTHOR

**Dear Reader,**

If you've made it to this page, I want to say something very simple, and very sincere: thank you.

Thank you for having the courage to begin. Thank you for staying with the hard chapters. And thank you for allowing me to walk beside you, even briefly, on your healing journey. I know how costly it is to revisit the pain. I also know how sacred it is to believe that healing is still possible.

You are not alone. Whatever brought you to this book—whether a fresh wound or a long-buried scar—please know that you are seen, loved, and held by the One who understands your story more deeply than anyone else ever could. Jesus doesn't stand at a distance from our suffering. He enters it. He weeps with us. And He walks us, step by step, toward restoration.

If your path still feels uncertain, that's okay. Healing is not a straight line. It's a holy journey. You don't have to have it all figured out. You just have to be willing to take the next faithful step. Christ will meet you there.

If this book has helped name your pain or opened the door to something new, I am deeply honored. That was my prayer when I wrote it.

And if you're still in the middle of the ache, hear this: you are not beyond hope. The God who redeems broken things is already at work in you.

With grace and gratitude,

Steve

Resource List:

# FINDING HELP
# BEYOND THE PAGES

Healing from trauma is not something we do alone. The journey often includes a combination of faith, community, counseling, and practical support. Below are a few trusted resources to help you continue forward.

## Emergency & Crisis Support

- 988 Suicide & Crisis Lifeline (U.S.): Dial 988 or visit 988lifeline.org

- Veterans Crisis Line: Dial 988 then press 1, or text 838255

- Crisis Text Line: Text HOME to 741741 (24/7 support)

## Christian Trauma and Counseling Resources

- American Association of Christian Counselors (AACC): www.aacc.net

- Focus on the Family Counseling Referrals: 1-855-771-HELP

- Faithful Counseling (online Christian therapy): www.faithfulcounseling.com

## Books and Ministries I Recommend

- *The Bronze Scar* by Dr Steve West

- *Try Softer* by Aundi Kolber

- *Wounded Healer* by Henri Nouwen

- *Soul Care* by Dr. Rob Reimer

- The ministry of *Reboot Recovery* (faith-based trauma healing) – www.rebootrecovery.com

## Veteran & First Responder Support

- Mighty Oaks Foundation – www.mightyoaksprograms.org

- Reboot Recovery for First Responders & Military – www.rebootrecovery.com

## Connect with Me

To share your story, request a speaking engagement, or stay connected, visit: www.drstevewest.com

Or reach out via email: steve@drstevewest.com

www.ingramcontent.com/pod-product-compliance
Lightning Source LLC
Chambersburg PA
CBHW060410130626
46555CB00005B/2017